"Christmas   198

Port Chester, New
York
10573
914 937-1334

METROPOLITAN OPERA GUILD
COMPOSER SERIES

VERDI

the Man and his Music

PAUL HUME

Picture Editor: Gerald Fitzgerald

E. P. DUTTON
in association with
METROPOLITAN OPERA GUILD
New York

Published 1977, in the United States by E. P. Dutton, a Division of Sequoia-Elsevier Publishing Company Inc., New York. All rights reserved under International and Pan-American Copyright conventions.

No part of this publication may be reproduced or transmitted in any form or by any means, electronic or mechanical, including photocopy, recording, or any information storage and retrieval system now known or to be invented, without permission in writing from the publisher, except by a reviewer who wishes to quote brief passages in connection with a review written for inclusion in a magazine, newspaper or broadcast. | Library of Congress Cataloging in Publication Data | Hume, Paul | Verdi | (The Metropolitan Opera Guild composer series) | 1. Verdi, Giuseppe, 1813–1901 2. Composers—Italy —Biography. I. Series: Metropolitan Opera Guild. The Metropolitan Opera Guild Composer series. | ML410.V4H74 782.1'092'4 [B] 77-5810 | ISBN: 0-525-22845-4 | Published simultaneously in Canada by Clarke, Irwin & Company Limited, Toronto and Vancouver | Picture Editor and Captions by Gerald Fitzgerald | Project Coordinator, Leslie Carola | Production director, David Zable | Text set by Pyramid Composition Company, Inc. | Display type set by Space Composers Group, Ltd. | Printed and bound by Dai Nippon Co., Ltd. | Designed by The Etheredges | 10 9 8 7 6 5 4 3 2 1 | First Edition

CONTENTS

FOREWORD

THE Metropolitan Opera Guild Composer Series is an introduction to the lives of major composers whose works form the backbone of the opera repertory. Though designed for the general public, these brief, authoritative, illustrated books are a valuable addition to the library of every music-lover.

The authors are well-known authorities whose names are familiar to a nationwide public through association with the Saturday afternoon intermission broadcasts from the Metropolitan Opera.

Photographs and documentation have been selected by Gerald Fitzgerald, associate editor of *Opera News,* the magazine of the Metropolitan Opera Guild, and editor of the annual Guild calendars from which many of the illustrations are drawn. The stories of the operas were compiled by Stephen Wadsworth of *Opera News*.

The series was conceived by Dario Soria, managing director of the Metropolitan Opera Guild, and planned in conjunction with Leslie Carola of the Guild and the editors of E. P. Dutton.

THE PUBLISHERS

ACKNOWLEDGMENTS

In writing this story of Verdi I have happily reread some of the great books that explore his life and music. No lover of Verdi can afford not to be well acquainted with the first two. All are of genuine interest. The Verdi Studies—Studi Verdiani—are valuable documents published at intervals by the Institute of Verdi Studies in Parma.

FRANK WALKER, *The Man Verdi*. Alfred A. Knopf, New York, 1962.

CHARLES OSBORNE, *The Complete Operas of Verdi*. Alfred A. Knopf, New York, 1970.

CARLO GATTI, *Verdi, the Man and His Music*. G. P. Putnam's Sons, London, 1955.

GEORGE MARTIN, *Verdi, His Music, Life and Times*. Dodd, Mead & Company, New York, 1963.

VINCENT SHEEAN, *Orpheus at Eighty*. Random House, New York, 1958.

PATRICK J. SMITH, *The Tenth Muse*. Alfred A. Knopf, New York, 1970.

Atti del II° Congresso Internazionale di Studi Verdiani, Parma, 1971.

JULIAN BUDDEN, *The Operas of Verdi: From Oberto to Rigoletto.* Praeger, New York, 1973.

Above all, remember the heart of Verdi, which beats in those operas and the Requiem.

Washington, D.C. New Year's Eve 1976   PAUL HUME

PICTURE CREDITS

VERDI

I

FROM LE RONCOLE TO LA SCALA

O<small>N</small> the night of February 17, 1859, Giuseppe Verdi's twenty-first opera, *Un Ballo in Maschera,* had its premiere in the Teatro Apollo in Rome. It was an immense success. The audience, in total agreement with Rome's music critics, was wildly enthusiastic. That night there was a new sound in their shouts of approval: Verdi's vociferous admirers were roaring "Viva Verdi!" with unprecedented fervor. The great man's name had become a symbol. Verdi meant to them not only the composer of their beloved *Rigoletto* and *Il Trovatore,* of *La Traviata* and the earlier successes, *Nabucco, Ernani* and *Macbeth.* The letters in the name V-E-R-D-I could also stand for Vittorio Emmanuele, Re d'Italia, and "Viva Verdi!" became a two-edged battle cry, a slogan that appeared on walls from one end of the country to the other. It was

Carlo and Luigia Verdi tended an inn at Le Roncole, a village near Busseto on the verdant plains of Emilia Romagna. In these modest surroundings on October 10, 1813, their only son, Giuseppe, was born. This painting of the inn by Achille Formis hangs in the La Scala Theater Museum

painted on banners, written on sidewalks, shouted out publicly. How could the Austrian police prove that those who shouted or scribbled it were not merely saluting the creator of Gilda, Violetta and Leonora?

Giuseppe Verdi's music had made him the most popular composer in Italy. His name, V-E-R-D-I, made him even more beloved in a country moving inexorably to throw off the foreign rule that had divided it for centuries, and to unite under Vittorio Emmanuele, then King of Sardinia. Before that year was over, Verdi was elected to an assembly in Parma. When the duchy voted to unit with Piedmont, it was Verdi who was chosen to carry the good news to the king. At the age of forty-six the man born on October 10, 1813, in the tiny town of Le Roncole, a short distance northwest of Parma on the road to Milan, had come a long way since the day his name had to be registered in French—Joseph Fortunin François instead of Giuseppe Fortunino Francesco—because the Parma region was controlled by the French.

The year after the composer's birth, Russian and Austrian troops involved in the power struggle then going on all over Europe were roaming through northern Italy in an attempt to run out the French. The world might easily have lost the genius of Verdi if his mother had not been a woman of common sense and fast footwork. When word came that a band of Russian soldiers was descending on Le Roncole, Verdi's mother, Luigia, grabbed her son and ran with him up into the bell tower of the church that stood across the road from the inn she and her husband operated. The soldiers came, killing and robbing some of the townspeople and even raping some of the women who had fled to the church for safety. But young Giuseppe and his mother escaped without harm. In this story, which was often repeated years later by Verdi's wife Giuseppina, the village church played its first major role in the young boy's life. The second was the sound of its organ, which so fascinated little Giuseppe that his father bought an old, beat-up spinet patched up by a neighbor so the boy could play on it. (He would keep the instrument all his life.)

It was not long before the church organist began giving him lessons. The world should remember the names of those generous enough to teach little children without the least idea that they may be furthering a great career. The organist who started Verdi on his long road to fame was Pietro Baistrocchi.

The boy made rapid progress. Although he was only twelve when Baistrocchi died, student replaced master as village organist, earning thirty-six lire a year, with bonuses for weddings and funerals. Earning this money involved more than playing the church organ. Two years earlier Giuseppe had been sent to live in the neighboring town of Busseto. His six years of employment in the church of Le Roncole required a six-mile round-trip walk every Sunday and feast day, a walk he often made barefoot in order to save shoe leather.

Carlo and Luigia Verdi's decision to pack the ten-year-old off to Busseto came about when the old priest who had taught the parish school in Le Roncole died. The suggestion that the obviously clever boy should be sent to greener educational pastures than those now available in his home town probably originated with Antonio Barezzi, a prosperous grocer and wine merchant of Busseto with whom Carlo Verdi did business.

Barezzi was Verdi's first great benefactor. He was like a second father to the boy—and eventually became his actual father-in-law. Although Giuseppe boarded with the village cobbler (for thirty *centesimi* a day), his life in Busseto revolved around the Barezzi household, a happy hotbed of musical activity. It was here that the town band, grandly named the Philharmonic Society, met for rehearsal, with Signor Barezzi variously performing on the flute, horn and clarinet or, if the occasion demanded, on the ophicleide.

Barezzi's high hopes for the little boy from Le Roncole were echoed by Giuseppe's music master, Ferdinando Provesi, organist and choirmaster of the Church of San Bartolomeo, director of the town music school and

the Philharmonic Society. Provesi's conviction that young Verdi was destined for a career in music was not shared by Don Pietro Seletti, the parish priest and Giuseppe's teacher of non-musical subjects. Don Pietro had no doubt that the intelligent boy was meant for the priesthood. The running battle between the two men ended abruptly one day when Giuseppe, substituting for a local organist, improvised so brilliantly that even Don Pietro saw the light. God, the honest priest was forced to admit, obviously intended the boy to be a musician.

Within four years Giuseppe had become the best pianist in the district. He was also teaching the younger pupils in the music school, continuing to play the organ at Le Roncole, copying parts for the Philharmonic Society, often directing their rehearsals—and composing a huge amount of music, usually for occasions in town when new music was needed.

When Verdi was forty, he wrote about his activities in those early years: "From my thirteenth to my eighteenth year (the age at which I went to Milan to study counterpoint) I wrote an assortment of pieces: marches for brass band by the hundred, perhaps as many little *sinfonie* that were used in church, in the theater or at concerts, five or six concertos and sets of variations for pianoforte, which I played myself at concerts, many serenades, cantatas (arias, duets, very many trios) and various pieces of church music, of which I remember only a Stabat Mater."

By the time Verdi was eighteen he had left his lodgings and moved into the Barezzi household, where he was treated as one of the family. The Barezzis had two sons and four daughters, one of whom, Margherita, was a few months younger than Verdi. Auburn-haired Margherita had been attracted to the young musician for years. Once she began to study piano and singing with him, they quickly fell in love. This was perfectly all right with Margherita's parents, but Barezzi wanted more for his future son-in-law than the music world of Busseto could provide. The

Today, in the room where Verdi was born, only a plaque and some colored streamers, the gift of neighboring towns, give relief to the rustic quarters—exposed hand-hewn beams, stucco walls, irregular brick flooring. Some period furniture can be seen in other rooms of the inn, now a tourist site

Elizabeth — Ego Carolus Arcari Praep.t Roncularum hora seconda pomeridiana diei dicti Baptizavi infantem natam hac mane prima luce ex Ioanne Antonio Giuffredi, et ex M.a Aloijsia Becchioni S.t Costantij conjugibus hujus Parox. cui impositum est nomen — M.a Elizabeth — Patrini fuere Ioseph Leurini f.s Antonij M.is et M.a Antonia Giuffredi f.lia Francisci, et uxor Ioannis Porcari ambo hujus Paraeciae. Ingior.

Anno Dni 1813 die 5.bris: — ad 47. m.o 1587 f.o ag.
Ego Carolus Arcari hodiernus Praepositus Roncularum hoc vespere Baptizavi Infantem natam hoc mane ex Dominico Orsi S.ti Hieronijmi; Iuliana Ferrari S.ti Con conjugibus hujus Paraecinae, cui impositum est nomen — M.a Aloijsia Patrini fuere Carolus Orsi f.us Hieronijmi hujus Paraeciae; et Aloijsia Ferrari f.a Antonii Paraeciae. Simorizei in quorum &c.

anno Dni 1813. die 11.a 8bris: — ad 48. m.o 1588 f.o 29
Ego Carolus Arcari Praep.s Roncularum hoc mane Baptizavi; Infantem natum heri vespere hora octava ex Carolo Verdi q.m Ioseph; et ex Aloijsia Utini f.a Caroli conjugibus hujus Paraeciae cui impositum est nomen — Ioseph Fortuninus Franciscus: — Patrini fuere D.us Petrus Cavali q.m Betici Barbara Bersani f. angeli amb hujus Paraeciae. Ingiorum &c.

merchant sent eighteen-year-old Verdi to Milan to apply for admission to the conservatory. His application was promptly denied. Verdi remained bitter about the denial all his life. Even in old age he wrote angrily to a friend, "In 1832, in June (I was not yet nineteen) I applied in writing to be admitted to the Milan Conservatory as a paying pupil. Moreover, I underwent a kind of examination at the conservatory, submitting some of my compositions and playing a piano piece before Basily, Piantanida, Angeleri and others, including old Rolla, to whom I had been recommended by my teacher at Busseto, Ferdinando Provesi. About a week later I went to Rolla, who said to me, 'Give up all idea of the conservatory; choose a teacher in the city, I suggest either Lavigna or Negro.' I heard nothing more from the conservatory. Nobody replied to my application. Nobody spoke to me, either before or after the examination, of the regulations."

This is not quite accurate, however, as Frank Walker points out. His application had in fact been returned to him: it was found among his papers after his death. In that application Verdi mentioned the fact that he was four years over the normal age limit. It is clear he was rejected for reasons that seemed good and sufficient to the school officials— because of the age discrepancy, because his piano playing was not up to conservatory standards, because he was a "foreigner" from Parma and because the conservatory classrooms and living space were overcrowded.

What Verdi did not mention in his resentful letter was a comment about his promise as a composer made by Basily, professor of composition. Basily's report to the director of the conservatory concluded with this cautious prediction: "As regards the compositions he presented as his own, I am in complete agreement with Signor Piantanida, teacher of counterpoint and vice-registrar, that if he applies himself attentively and patiently to studying the rules of counterpoint, he will be able to control

France ruled the Duchy of Parma in 1813, so Verdi's birth certificate reads Joseph, not Giuseppe (top). During skirmishes between French and Austrian forces, Verdi's mother hid with her baby in the bell tower of the church across the way from their inn. There Verdi later served as acolyte and organist

the genuine imagination he shows himself to possess and thus turn out creditably as a composer."

At this discouraging point Antonio Barezzi proved to be one of history's most generous and far-seeing benefactors. Picking up the suggestion that Verdi should remain in Milan and study composition, Barezzi agreed to underwrite most of the costs for four years of private study there. (He even added a gift of a square piano.)

Barezzi hoped that somehow Giuseppe's father, Carlo, would be

Verdi moved to Busseto to further his musical studies. In time he lived in the home of his patron, Antonio Barezzi (right), a supplier of goods to his father; the local Philharmonic Society rehearsed in Barezzi's salon (below right). Young Verdi is shown below giving a lesson to a Countess Zaccaria

able to send enough money for clothing. Additional financing came—not without considerable haggling—from the Monte di Pietà e d'Abbondanza, an institution that gave money to poor children of talent.

Verdi's teacher of composition was Vincenzo Lavigna, a protégé of Paisiello and chief conductor at La Scala. Just how good a teacher for Verdi was he? Verdi himself supplies a partial answer: "Lavigna was very strong in counterpoint, a bit of a pedant, and had no use for any other music than that of Paisiello. I remember that in a sinfonia I wrote, he corrected all the scoring in the manner of Paisiello. 'I should be in a fix,' I said to myself—and from that moment I did not show him any more of my original compositions, and in the three years spent with him I did not do anything but canons and fugues, fugues and canons of all sorts. *No one taught me orchestration or how to treat dramatic music.*" (Italics added.) Where and how did Verdi learn these things? He taught himself, this man whose music dramas were to become the most beloved and most frequently performed operas in the world.

Lavigna also did something for Verdi that was to have the greatest consequences: he told his young pupil to take a season ticket for the opera. (For this, too, the peerless Barezzi provided the funds.) Before he had studied a year in Milan, Verdi knew his music was going to be written for the theater.

It took him less than three years, a relatively short detour, to convert ambition into reality and begin the career he would follow, with single-minded devotion, for over half a century.

When Verdi completed his studies in Milan, he returned to Busseto, married Margherita Barezzi and served three years as organist in San Bartolomeo. (Even that humble position had not come to him without prolonged and occasionally bloodcurdling differences of opinion among the townsfolk of Busseto.) But his success in Milan both as conductor and student of composition had already led to an operatic commission from the Teatro Filodrammatico. The question of which opera he first worked on for the project remains a complex historical mystery; in any case, *Oberto, Conte di San Bonifacio* was begun in Busseto in the winter of 1837 and completed early the next year. A Milanese journalist named Piazza supplied a not too distinguished libretto to the novice composer. (It was later augmented by Temistocle Solera.)

Although the production by the Teatro Filodrammatico fell through, the director of La Scala, Bartolomeo Merelli, decided to stage the work as a charity benefit in the spring of 1839. The illness of tenor Napoleone Moriani caused the cancellation of the opera. Influences were worked on Merelli that caused the piece to be rescheduled for the regular season. On November 17, 1839, the first performance of an opera by Giuseppe Verdi was presented on the stage at La Scala.

Oberto was well received, played fourteen performances and was bought for 2,000 lire by the great publishing house of Ricordi, thus launching a historic artistic and business collaboration.

It all should have been so happy, this magnificently promising beginning of a career. It was not. The events surrounding the completion and premiere of *Oberto* were played out under a cloud of intense personal tragedy in the life of the composer. In August 1838, just after the score was finished, Virginia, the young couple's first child, died. A son, Icilio, was born in July 1838—and died fifteen months later, shortly before the opening of *Oberto*. June 1840 brought the greatest tragedy of all: Margherita Verdi died of encephalitis at the age of twenty-seven. Verdi's world, so full of joy and promise, had fallen into ruins. Less than three months after the death of his wife, his second opera—ironically it was a comic piece, *Un Giorno di Regno*—failed dismally. "With mind tormented by my domestic misfortunes," he wrote, "embittered by the failure of my work, I was convinced I could find no consolation in my art and decided never to compose again."

Three factors in his life would soon reverse this decision. They were Bartolomeo Merelli, *Nabucco* and Giuseppina Strepponi.

II

"VA, PENSIERO"

Bartolomeo Merelli was, as we have seen, the impresario of La Scala, then as now Europe's leading opera theater. Giuseppina Strepponi was one of Italy's star sopranos. Born on September 8, 1815, she showed such pronounced musical talent that, unlike Verdi, she was admitted to the Milan Conservatory even though in 1830 she too was over the age limit. By 1838 Strepponi was being wildly cheered for her singing of Lucia and Norma and in *I Puritani.* No wonder that when *Oberto* was ready for production, Verdi was pleased that so popular a singer would be its leading soprano. When the illness of the tenor Moriani canceled the benefit performance, it was she who urged Merelli to accept the work for the coming season at La Scala. Once the impresario had seen the success of *Oberto,* he contracted with Verdi

Verdi went to Milan to study at the age of eighteen. Denied admission by the conservatory that now bears his name, he worked privately. By 1839, when he was only twenty-six, his first opera had been accepted for production by the city's musical mecca, the Teatro alla Scala, seen at left in a painting by Inganni

OBERTO
CONTE DI S. BONIFACIO

DRAMMA IN DUE ATTI

DA RAPPRESENTARSI

NELL' I. R. TEATRO ALLA SCALA

L' AUTUNNO 1839.

DAMIANO MUONI
Libri, Disegni, Stampe, Ritratti
Pergamene, Manoscritti, Autografi

Milano

PER GASPARE TRUFFI

UN GIORNO
DI REGNO

MELODRAMMA GIOCOSO

IN DUE ATTI

DA RAPPRESENTARSI

NELL'I. R. TEATRO ALLA SCALA

L' AUTUNNO DEL 1840

DAMIANO MUONI
Libri, Disegni, Stampe, Ritratti
Pergamene, Manoscritti, Autografi

Milano

PER GASPARE TRUFFI
M.DCCC.XL.

Oberto, *staged at La Scala on November 17, 1839, united Verdi with the House of Ricordi, Italy's leading music publisher. A moderate success, the work earned him a contract to pen three more operas. First of these was a comedy,* Un Giorno di Regno, *a fiasco at its world premiere at La Scala on September 5, 1840*

for three more operas, to be completed at intervals of eight months. Even when the ghastly emotional crisis arose in Verdi's life, Merelli did not abandon "his" new composer. Whether or not he knew he was practicing amateur psychology, Merelli's instincts were sound when he sent for the composer, whom he had known for less than a year. Verdi has left a vivid account of what happened:

"Merelli sent for me and treated me like a capricious child. He would not allow me to be discouraged by the failure of one opera, and so on. But I insisted, until finally he gave me the contract back and said, 'Listen, Verdi! I can't force you to compose. But my faith in you is undiminished. Who knows whether one day you may not decide to write again? In which case, if you give me two months' notice before the beginning of a season, I promise your opera shall be performed.' I thanked him, but these words did not suffice to alter my decision, and I left.

"I took rooms in Milan, in the Corsia de' Servi. I had lost heart, and no longer thought about music; but one winter evening, as I was leaving the Galleria de Cristoforis, I ran into Merelli, on his way to the theater. It was snowing heavily. Taking me by the arm, he asked me to accompany him to his office at La Scala. On the way we talked, and he told me he was having difficulty over a new opera. He had commissioned Nicolai, who was, however, dissatisfied with the new libretto.

" 'Just think,' said Merelli, 'a libretto by Solera! Stupendous! Magnificent! Extraordinary! Effective, grandiose dramatic situations and beautiful verses!' . . . Meanwhile," Verdi continues, "Merelli picked up another manuscript and, showing it to me, exclaimed, 'Look, here is Solera's libretto. Such a beautiful subject, and now it's turned down. Take it and read it.'

" 'What on earth should I do with it? No, no, I don't want to read any librettos.'

" 'Come on, it won't bite you. Read it and then bring it back to me.'

And he gave me the manuscript. It was written on large paper in big letters, as was customary then. I rolled it up, said good-bye to Merelli and went home.

"On the way I felt a kind of indefinable uneasiness, a deep sadness, an anguish that filled my heart. When I got home, I threw the manuscript on the table with a violent gesture and stood staring at it. It had fallen

Modern stagings of Verdi's first two operas are rare. La Scala revived Oberto *in 1951 with Gianni Poggi, Tancredi Pasero and Ebe Stignani (right), and Bologna staged it in 1977 with Angeles Gulin and Viorica Cortez (below left).* Un Giorno di Regno *turned up in Como in 1973 with Maria Casula, Franca Fabbri, Ibrahim Moubayed (below right)*

open, and without realizing it I gazed at the page and read the line 'Và, pensiero, sull'ali dorate' "—Fly, thought, on wings of gold.

"I glanced through the following verses and was deeply moved, particularly since they were almost a paraphrase of the Bible, which I have always enjoyed reading.

"I read one passage, then another. Then, resolute in my determination never to compose again, I forced myself to close the book and go to bed. But *Nabucco* kept running through my mind, and I couldn't sleep. I got up and read the libretto, not once but two or three times, so that by morning I knew it almost by heart. Even so, I was determined to stick to my decision, and that day I returned to the theater and handed the manuscript back to Merelli.

" 'Beautiful, isn't it?' he said.

" 'Very beautiful.'

" 'Well then, set it to music.'

" 'Certainly not. I wouldn't think of it.'

" 'Set it to music! Set it to music!' And with that he took the libretto, thrust it into my overcoat pocket, grabbed me by the shoulders and not only pushed me out of the room but locked the door in my face.

"What was I to do? I went home with *Nabucco* in my pocket. One day a verse, the next day another, at one time a note, at another a phrase. Little by little the opera was written."

On March 9, 1842, *Nabucco* was produced.

"With this opera it is fair to say my artistic career began," Verdi wrote. "And in spite of the difficulties I had to contend with, *Nabucco* was born under a lucky star." He tells us that "the first scene in the temple produces such an effect that the audience applauded for ten minutes." In this Verdi score is heard for the first time the kind of political overtone that was to bring the audience in Rome to its feet that February

In 1836 Verdi married the titian-haired Margherita Barezzi, daughter of his patron. Their wedded joy was brief: two offspring, Virginia and Icilio, died during infancy, and Margherita herself succumbed to encephalitis in 1840. This, with the failure of Un Giorno di Regno, *plunged Verdi into bitter despair*

La Scala's director, Bartolomeo Merelli, and the soprano Giuseppina Strepponi (above) helped Verdi, unproductive for a year, regain confidence. Merelli literally thrust a new libretto, Nabucco, into his hands. The prima donna, who was to sing the role of Abigaille, years later became Verdi's wife. Nabucco was first staged at the Metropolitan Opera in 1960 with Rosalind Elias, Bonaldo Giaiotti, Cornell MacNeil, Leonie Rysanek and Eugenio Fernandi (top right), but it has been heard regularly at La Scala (below right) since its triumphant world premiere, on March 9, 1842—shown here in a 1958 production with Ettore Bastianini as Nabucco and Anita Cerquetti as Abigaille

G. VERDI

NABUCCO

OPERA COMPLETA
PER
CANTO
E
PIANOFORTE

EDIZIONI RICORDI

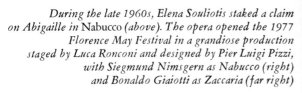

*During the late 1960s, Elena Souliotis staked a claim
on Abigaille in* Nabucco *(above). The opera opened the 1977
Florence May Festival in a grandiose production
staged by Luca Ronconi and designed by Pier Luigi Pizzi,
with Siegmund Nimsgern as Nabucco (right)
and Bonaldo Giaiotti as Zaccaria (far right)*

night seventeen years later: it is the celebrated chorus fashioned out of the line he saw the day he threw the manuscript on the table. So moving is the soaring melody of this chorus, "Và, pensiero," that the audience demanded and received an encore, in spite of a law forbidding encores— a vain move on the part of the Austrians to prevent patriotic demonstrations against the absentee rulers.

With that one chorus Verdi became, however involuntarily, a leading figure in the movement toward a free, united Italy. Any Italian hearing the chorus heard not the captive Hebrews, "in chains, at forced labor" as the libretto puts it, but Italians, captive under an Austrian yoke. "Oh, my country, so lovely and lost! Oh, remembrance so dear and so fraught with despair" is not the song of the Babylonian captives centuries earlier. For Italian audiences in the 1840s it was the song of hope for the day when Italy would be free. To *that* day was the "thought, on wings of gold" directed to fly.

Nabucco carried Verdi's music to other major opera theaters in Europe and on the American continents. Paris and London heard it in 1845 and 1846. It ran into a censorship problem in London, where the law barred Biblical subjects from the stage. So *Nabucco* appeared as "Nino, Re d'Assyria," and all the Hebrews were changed, as if in an Old Testament miracle, into Babylonians!

With *Nabucco* Verdi engaged in the first of what became an almost unbroken line of arguments with his librettists. His sense of what was effective theatrically was uneven, but he had a better feeling for the opera stage than most of his writers. He tells of an encounter with the librettist:

"I remember an amusing scene I had with Solera a little earlier. In the third act he had written a love duet for Fenena and Ismaele. I didn't like it, as it held up the action and seemed to me to detract somewhat from the Biblical grandeur of the drama. One morning I said so to Solera. But he was loath to agree, not because he thought the comment unfair but because it annoyed him to revise anything he had written. We argued about it, and both stood firm. He asked what I wanted to replace the duet, and I suggested the prophecy of Zaccaria. He thought that wasn't a bad idea, and with a few ifs and buts said he'd think about it and then write it. That was no good for me, for I knew that a good many days would pass before Solera sat down to write a verse. So I locked the door, put the key in my pocket and said, half seriously and half flippantly, 'You're not leaving here until you've written the prophecy. Here's the Bible, you have the words already made.'

"Solera, who had a violent temper, didn't care for my joke. An angry look appeared in his eye, and I was nervous for a moment, for the poet was certainly big enough to put an obstinate composer in his place. But suddenly he sat at the table, and in a quarter of an hour the prophecy was written."

Despite its garbled libretto, the chronicle of an Italian crusade during the eleventh-century, I Lombardi alla Prima Crociata *earned a frenzied reception at its world premiere at La Scala on February 11, 1843. Four years later, a revision was produced by Verdi in Paris under the title* Jérusalem

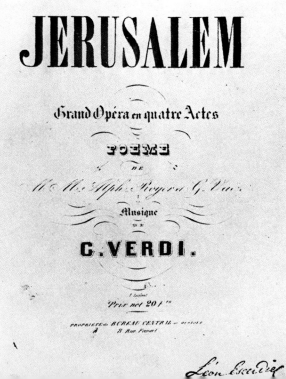

In the years to come, Verdi would more than once wish for a locked room if not indeed a loaded gun as he continued to labor and argue with Solera, Piave and Cammarano, Scribe and Somma. Only when he reached the two last, and greatest, of all his operas would he work with a man whose genius as librettist was the equal of Verdi's as composer.

There is a significant psychological episode in *Nabucco* that will recur frequently in Verdi's operas. It is the duet for Nabucco and Abigaille, father and daughter. This is the forerunner of the father-daughter duets that ennoble later operas: the scenes between Luisa Miller and her father; Rigoletto and Gilda; the elder Germont, who assumes a father's role, and Violetta; the powerful scene between Simon Boccanegra and his long-lost

Performances of I Lombardi alla Prima Crociata *or* Jérusalem *are infrequent today. One of the most notable recent productions of the former was mounted at the Rome Opera in 1969 by director Giorgio De Lullo and designer Pier Luigi Pizzi. Cast in the demanding soprano lead, Giselda, was Renata Scotto (below)*

daughter, Amelia; and that moving third-act confrontation between Amonasro and Aida. It is hardly playing at psychoanalysis to remember in these scenes the anguish of a father whose only children died in infancy. Surely some of the sweet affection of these pages has roots in the personal tragedy that left ineradicable lines on Verdi's face.

Encouraged by the success of *Nabucco,* Verdi began to work at an awesome rate of speed. In the nine years between *Nabucco* and *Rigoletto* (1842 to 1851) he would write fourteen operas.

"Thanks for remembering your poor friend, condemned continually to scribble musical notes," he wrote a well-wisher during the composition of *Attila*. "God save the ears of every good Christian from having to

29

listen to them! Accursed notes! How am I, physically and spiritually? Physically I am well, but my mind is black, always black, and will be so until I have finished with this career that I abhor. And afterward? It's useless to delude oneself. It will always be black. Happiness does not exist for me."

It seems unlikely that Verdi truly "abhorred" the career he practiced until he was over eighty years old. This literary effusion—and many more like it—followed a pattern established as early as the days of *Un Giorno di Regno*. Verdi at work was consistently plagued by enough aches and ailments to fill a textbook of psychosomatic medicine. Headaches, rheumatism, flu, gastritis in varied forms, depression and other ills made the poor composer's life a misery, for it was true then as now that no matter what the cause of the symptoms, mental or physical, the effects are equally devastating to the patient!

Yet he worked like a demon during what he called his "galley years," and they produced far more successes than failures. *I Lombardi* had a triumphant premiere at La Scala in 1843. The next year would see the success of *I Due Foscari* and *Ernani*. 1845 brought *Giovanna d'Arco* and *Alzira*, while 1847 saw no less than three premieres: *Macbeth, Jérusalem* (a revision of *I Lombardi,* written for Paris) and *I Masnadieri,* written for Her Majesty's Theater as a vehicle for the reigning operatic queen of London, Jenny Lind. 1849 was the year of *Luisa Miller* and *La Battaglia di Legnano.*

All this activity took a fearful toll. Verdi's creative attention was constantly being distracted from work in progress by the demands of theatrical production, since he supervised not only premieres but also as many revivals of older works as he could. It made for a frantic pace. Immediately after the first *Foscari* performance in Rome, for example, he raced back to Milan to prepare not only the premiere of *Giovanna d'Arco*

Ernani, based on Victor Hugo's melodrama about honor, was the first of five operas Verdi composed for the Teatro la Fenice in Venice. It was also the first of eleven collaborations with librettist Francesco Maria Piave. Seen at left are Leontyne Price as Elvira and Leonard Warren as Don Carlo, her suitor

but a revival of *I Lombardi.* Emmanuele Muzio, Verdi's new secretary and flunky-of-all-trades (the sort of willing doormat found near all great musicians), gives us a clear picture of the composer at work on the *Lombardi* revival. He "shouted like a madman," Muzio reports, "and stamped his feet so much he looked as though he were playing the organ. He sweated so profusely that the perspiration dripped on the score." But Muzio adds that "at his glance, at a sign from him, the singers, chorus and orchestra seemed to be touched by an electric spark."

Ernani, one of the 1844 operas, marked two important firsts in Verdi's career. It was his first opera to be produced at La Fenice in Venice, Italy's second-ranking house. The critical Venetian audiences hailed the thirty-year-old composer wholeheartedly, and Verdi was satisfied with the production except in one particular: "It is impossible," he wrote a friend, "to sing flatter than Loewe did last night." Since Sophie Loewe, the first Elvira, had been angry at the composer for refusing to give her a florid showpiece to end the opera, it is possible her mood depressed her pitch. (In spite of their differences, it was Loewe, two years later, who would create the role of Odabella in *Attila,* a second Fenice premiere.)

Ernani's second distinction was its librettist. This was the first of Verdi's texts written by the poet Francesco Maria Piave, the man Verdi would bully and badger, beg and cajole for the next eighteen years. Piave would furnish Verdi with nine librettos, by far the greatest number supplied by any one writer. Among them would be some of the composer's greatest works: *Rigoletto, La Traviata, Simon Boccanegra, La Forza del Destino.*

When Piave began the book for *Ernani* he was a complete novice at writing librettos. Verdi informed him bluntly that in case of disagreement he would always settle the arguments personally and in his own favor, an attitude he steadfastly maintained for life. On the whole, however, Piave did a fair job in the tough business of making Victor Hugo's revolutionary

When Ernani *entered the repertory of the Metropolitan Opera, in 1903, Marcella Sembrich sang Elvira's "Ernani, involami." Later heroines included Rosa Ponselle and Zinka Milanov. Seen here in the 1965 revival are Leontyne Price as Elvira, Jerome Hines as Silva and Franco Corelli as the noble bandit of the title*

Hernani fit the requirements of the opera stage. In writing "Ernani, involami" he gave Verdi a text for the first of his arias to become a staple for audience-whistling around the world. It stands with the melody of "Và, pensiero" as one of his greatest early inspirations.

The year after the triumph of *Ernani* Verdi wrote a lesser piece, based on the story of the heroic Maid of Orleans. The musical sycophant Emmanuele Muzio went into ecstasies over the work and declared that if Joan of Arc had not immortalized herself by her deeds, Verdi's music would have done it for her. Few people agree with him, though the score of *Giovanna d'Arco* became a great favorite among the organ grinders of Italy.

I Due Foscari, which concerns a power struggle in the Foscari clan of fifteenth-century Venice, was first heard in Rome in 1844, when Verdi was well launched on his "galley years," turning out fifteen operas in a single decade. Prima donna at the premiere was a Verdi favorite, Marianna Barbieri-Nini (below)

I DUE FOSCARI.

TRAGEDIA LIRICA IN TRE ATTI.

DA RAPPRESENTARSI

NEL

REAL TEATRO S. CARLO.

NAPOLI,
Dalla Tipografia Flautina
1845.

Giovanna d'Arco is interesting historically rather than musically, as the last Verdi opera to premiere at La Scala for twenty-five years. These were years in which Verdi's fame brought demands for the first performance of his works from opera houses all over Europe, to say nothing of Cairo. But not until 1872, when *Aida* was heard in Milan (not as a world premiere but simply as a European debut), did Verdi rescind his hostile determination not to give Scala another "first."

What had happened to turn the outraged composer against the world's foremost opera house, scene of his first great triumphs? Verdi explained it to his publisher, Giovanni Ricordi. "I approve the contract you have drawn up for my new opera, *Macbeth,*" he wrote on December

The Lyric Opera of Chicago revived I Due Foscari *in 1972 with Katia Ricciarelli (below) as Lucrezia, Barbieri-Nini's role. The production, by director Giorgio De Lullo with décor by Pier Luigi Pizzi, had been borrowed from Rome's Teatro dell' Opera and was seen during the company's 1967 New York visit*

29, 1846, "which will be produced at Florence during the coming Lent, and I agree to your making use of it, but on condition you not allow any performances of *Macbeth* at La Scala.

"I have had enough examples to convince me that here they can't or don't want to mount an opera properly, especially my own. I cannot forget how very badly they staged *I Lombardi, Ernani, I Due Foscari* . . . I have another example, *Attila,* before my eyes now. . . . I ask you whether this opera could be staged worse, in spite of a good cast. . . .

"I repeat, therefore, that I cannot and will not allow any performances of this *Macbeth* at La Scala, at least not until things have taken a turn for the better. I feel it my duty to warn you, for your guidance, that the condition I am now imposing for *Macbeth* will henceforth be imposed for all my operas."

The complaint about *Foscari* referred to the fact that in staging it at La Scala, Merelli had reversed the order of the second and third acts!

Once again the Fenice in Venice witnessed a Verdi triumph in the

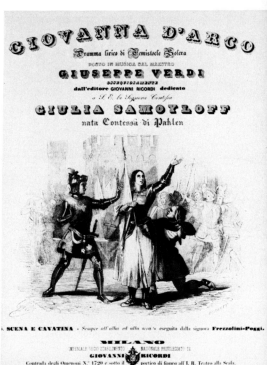

Giovanna d'Arco, *first given at La Scala in 1845, is Verdi's*
version of the St. Joan legend, freely adapted from Schiller's
Maid of Orleans. *In 1972 the opera was revived at La Fenice in*
Venice by director Alberto Fassini and designer Pier Luigi
Samaritani, with Katia Ricciarelli as Giovanna (left). Above
is the Teatro San Carlo of Naples, site of the premiere of two
*subsequent Verdi operas—*Alzira *(1845) and* Luisa Miller *(1849)*

premiere of *Attila,* an opera that reinforced Verdi's coming role as a leader of the Risorgimento. The subject had been in his mind for several years. He was fascinated with the possibilities of scenes involving the king of the Huns and a pope, the eventual founding of the city of Venice and the symbolisms centering around an army marching on Italy.

By the time Verdi got into the work, he was entering one of his worst periods of depression and nearing a point of almost total physical collapse. He wrote in bed, in what he called "an almost dying condition." This condition was hardly improved by the frequent blood-lettings recommended by his physicians. (Perhaps some of the weakness in the score of *Attila* can be attributed to his physical fatigue while writing it.) In spite of all this, the opera had a wildly successful opening on March 17, 1846.

Early in the prologue Verdi and his librettist, Solera, produced a mighty line that struck fire in the soul of all Italy. It occurs in the first scene, when the Roman general Ezio visits Attila and secretly proposes a pact. In a sweeping Verdian phrase Ezio sings, "Avrai tu l'universo, resti l'Italia a me"—"You take the universe, but leave Italy to me." When the baritone Constantini sang that line, the audience shouted, "A noi! l'Italia a noi!" Leave Italy to us!

Considering the problems Verdi increasingly encountered with censors, it is astounding that this line got by the Austrian watchdogs. But it did, and in the shortest time became an Italian rallying cry. At almost the same time Angelo Mariani, conducting a performance of *Nabucco* in Milan, was bawled out by the police commissioner, who threatened him with arrest because his conducting had given Verdi's music "an expression too rebellious and hostile to the Imperial Government."

With the successful premiere of *Attila* Verdi's health gave way entirely. His doctors ordered him to stop all work, to do nothing but rest for six months. Desperately weak, Verdi had no inclination to do anything

Alzira was loosely adapted from a Voltaire tragedy about Peru during the Spanish conquest. Verdi judged his music perhaps too severely: "really ugly." In a flamboyant 1967 revival staged by Sandro Sequi at the Rome Opera, Virginia Zeani as Alzira (left) had plumage more than equal to a costume sketch from Verdi's day

else. He gave himself up to a listless, irritable kind of life, in complete contrast to the hectic pace that had preceded it. But during the enforced period of rest Verdi gradually overcame both the physical weakness that had knocked him out and the psychological lethargy that had kept him from thinking about work.

Once he was able to work, the first opera to capture his imagination was the first of three that would link the names Verdi and Shakespeare. At the risk of bringing on serious and unprovable arguments among ardent Verdians, a good case can be made for the proposition that as *Otello* and *Falstaff,* his last two operas, are the greatest of all Verdi gave us, so is *Macbeth,* in its amazing psychological and musical insights, the greatest of his early operas.

Attila, a patriotic piece about the fifth-century invasion of Italy by the Huns, dates from 1846. Shown at left is Jerome Hines in the title role; at right, Leyla Gencer as Odabella, the spirit of Italian womanhood, does in the foreign invader, Nicolai Ghiaurov as Attila

III

MACBETH

As he did several times during his creative career, Verdi now began working on two operas at the same time: *Macbeth,* which fascinated him, and a version of Schiller's play *Die Räuber,* which became *I Masnadieri.* The first would have its premiere at the Pergola Theater in Florence. The second was to be Verdi's first and only London opening.

The name of Piave appears as the librettist for *Macbeth.* But Shakespeare was a lifelong enthusiasm of Verdi's. He made his own decisions on which scenes from the play he would use, and before letting Piave begin work Verdi himself wrote out an entire libretto in Italian, asking Piave only to turn it into verse. Nothing wounded Verdi more sorely than the suggestion of one critic that the composer did not know his Shake-

Verdi undertook three operas drawn from Shakespeare plays—
Macbeth, Otello *and* Falstaff. *The first, dating from 1847,*
shows Verdi's awareness of drama and is remarkably free from operatic
convention. In 1964 at the Metropolitan Opera, Macbeth and
his Lady were Cornell MacNeil and Brigit Nilsson (left)

speare. "Oh, there they are greatly mistaken," he wrote to his French publisher, Léon Escudier. "It may be that I did not do *Macbeth* justice, but to say I do not know, I do not understand and do not feel Shakespeare, no, by God, no! He is my favorite poet. I have known him from my childhood and read and reread him continually."

In another letter Verdi left one of the most convincing proofs of his consummate instincts and knowledge not only of singers and voices but of stage direction and orchestration.

"I understand you are rehearsing *Macbeth*," he wrote to Salvatore Cammarano, his librettist for four operas and also a producer. "As this opera interests me more than my others, please allow me to say a few words about it. Mme. Tadolini, I believe, is to sing Lady Macbeth, and I am astonished that she should have undertaken the part. You know how highly I regard Mme. Tadolini, and so does she, but for the sake of us all I feel I must say that her qualities are too fine for this role. This may sound absurd, but Mme. Tadolini is a handsome woman with a beautiful face, and I want Lady Macbeth to be ugly and evil. Mme. Tadolini sings to perfection, and I don't want Lady Macbeth to sing at all. Mme. Tadolini has a wonderful voice, clear, flexible and strong, while Lady Macbeth's voice should be hard, stifled and dark. Mme. Tadolini has the voice of an angel, and Lady Macbeth's should be that of a devil. Please bring these comments to the notice of the directors, of Maestro Mercadante, who will understand my ideas better than anyone, and of Mme. Tadolini herself. Do what you think best. Tell them the most important numbers in the opera are the duet between Macbeth and Lady Macbeth and the Sleepwalking Scene. If these two numbers fail, then the entire opera will fail. And these two numbers definitely must not be sung. They must be acted and declaimed, with hollow, masked voices. Otherwise it will make no effect.

"The orchestra *con sordini,*" Verdi went on. "The stage extremely dark. In the third act, the apparitions of the kings (I have seen this in London) must take place behind a special opening at the back, with a thin ash-colored veil in front of it. The kings must not be puppets but eight men of flesh and blood. The spot they pass over must be a kind of mound, and you should be able to see them ascend and descend. The stage must be completely dark, especially when the caldron disappears, with light only where the kings appear. The music from underneath the stage will have to be reinforced for the large San Carlo Theater. But take care there are no trumpets or trombones. The sound must seem faraway, muffled, so it must be composed of bass clarinets, bassoons, contrabassoons and nothing else."

For a soprano with the voice of a devil, Verdi turned to Marianna Barbieri-Nini. She in her turn has left us a vivid description of the composer's working methods and his inexorable demands that perfection, or its nearest counterpart, must be attained. Barbieri-Nini says, "And imagine this. The evening of the final rehearsal, with the theater full of guests, Verdi made the artists put on their costumes, and when he insisted on something, woe betide those who contradicted him. When we were dressed and ready, with the orchestra in the pit and the chorus already onstage, Verdi beckoned to me and Varesi to follow him into the wings. We did so, and he explained that he wanted us to come out into the foyer for another piano rehearsal of that wretched duet.

" 'Maestro,' I protested, 'we are already in our Scottish costumes. How can we?'

" 'Put cloaks over them.'

"Varesi, annoyed at this strange request, dared to raise his voice: 'But, for God's sake, we've already rehearsed it a hundred and fifty times.'

" 'I wouldn't say that if I were you, for within half an hour it will be a hundred and fifty-one.'

"But even Varesi gave in, and the one hundred and fifty-first rehearsal took place, while inside the theater the audience clamored impatiently."

The premiere of *Macbeth* so excited the spectators that they called the composer before the curtain thirty-eight times. Barbieri-Nini, glorying in the huge ovation that greeted her Sleepwalking Scene, realized the value of Verdi's hard-headed methods.

"The storm of applause had not yet died down," she recalled, "and I was standing in my dressing room, trembling and exhausted, when the door flew open—I was already half undressed—and Verdi stood before me. He gesticulated, and his lips moved as if he wanted to speak out but

At the Metropolitan Opera in 1973, Macbeth and his Lady were sung by Sherrill Milnes and Martina Arroyo (left), with Grace Bumbry also as the villainess (above). In 1975 at La Scala, Milan, Giorgio Strehler staged a production with Piero Cappuccilli and Shirley Verrett, shown at top right in the banquet scene. Bottom right, the Met staging of the refugee chorus

could not utter a word. Between tears and laughter, I too could say nothing. But I saw that his eyes were red. He squeezed my hand very tightly and rushed out. That moment of real feeling repaid me many times over for the months of hard work and continuous agitation."

The opera Verdi had begun to sketch out before he got to work on *Macbeth* would take him to England in the spring of 1847. The July 22 opening of *I Masnadieri* was one of the most extraordinary nights in the history of the London theater. An opera written especially for Her Majesty's Theater by Giuseppe Verdi, and conducted by the composer—this was in itself an enormous coup. That the leading role was sung by Jenny Lind, the reigning operatic queen of London and the Continent, made the evening a social as well as musical smash. Lind was the special favorite

of Queen Victoria and Prince Albert. Both of them were in Her Majesty's Theater that night, together with the whole of Parliament and every other member of London society who could make it through the famous "Jenny Lind crush" that happened every time the Swedish soprano set foot on the stage of Her Majesty's.

Muzio, obviously awed by the quantity of blue blood in the house, wrote, "From the overture to the finale there was nothing but applause, Evviva's recalls and encores. As soon as Verdi appeared in the orchestra pit, applause broke out and continued for a quarter of an hour. Before it had finished, the Queen and Prince Albert, her consort, the Queen Mother and the Duke of Cambridge, uncle of the Queen, the Prince of Wales, son of the Queen, and all the royal family and a countless number

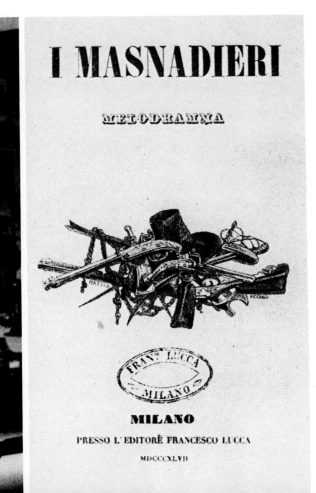

The plays of Friedrich Schiller provided source material for four Verdi works—Giovanna d'Arco, I Masnadieri *(The Robbers),* Luisa Miller *and* Don Carlos. *The second of these, a rousing tale of German highwaymen, was first given in London at Her Majesty's Theatre during July of 1847. Verdi himself conducted, as he had at the premiere of* Macbeth, *and his prima donna was the Swedish nightingale, Jenny Lind, whose voice Verdi found less than perfect. Shown at far left is a scene from the production of* I Masnadieri *that opened the 1972-73 season at Rome's Teatro dell'Opera*

of lords and dukes had arrived." Most of the London critics shared the enthusiasm of the royal family for *I Masnadieri*. The exception was the splendidly acerbic Henry Chorley, who announced flatly, "We take this to be the worst opera which has been given in our time at Her Majesty's Theater. Verdi is finally rejected. The field is open for an Italian composer."

London awed and delighted the man from Le Roncole. "It isn't a city," he wrote, "it's a world. Its size, the richness and beauty of the streets, the cleanliness of the houses, all this is incomparable." His comments are strikingly like those of Joseph Haydn over half a century earlier.

"One stands amazed," he went on, "and feels insignificant when, in the midst of all this splendor, one surveys the Bank of England and the docks. Who can resist the people? The surroundings and the country outside London are marvelous. But I do not like many of the English customs, or rather they do not suit us Italians."

After those final lines it is not hard to see why Verdi turned down an offer from the impresario Lumley to come back to London as musical director of Her Majesty's Theater at a very large salary, and to compose a new opera for that theater each year for ten years. With little enthusiasm Verdi rejected the terms. Whatever they were, over and above Lumley's "very large salary," that was the end of the idea.

Having conducted the first two performances of *I Masnadieri*, Verdi turned the baton over to Michael Balfe (composer of *The Bohemian Girl*) and went back to Paris, where he had stayed for a few days en route to London. Here he would revise *I Lombardi* into *Jérusalem* and prepare the premiere. He had, in addition, a compelling reason for this return visit to the City of Light. Before he left it, a magnificent change would have come into a life which, in spite of professional success, had for many years been an essentially joyless one.

The soprano and tenor stars of the 1972 revival of I Masnadieri *at the Teatro dell'Opera in Rome were Ilva Ligabue as Amalia and Gianni Raimondi as her lover, Carlo (left). One of the high points of Verdi's score is the overture, which contains an extended passage for solo cello that requires great virtuosity*

IV

GIUSEPPINA

GIUSEPPINA Strepponi and Verdi had met in Milan early in the composer's career. It was the generous-hearted Strepponi, as we have seen, who persuaded Merelli to present the young mans' first opera at La Scala. Again it was Strepponi who championed the cause of *Nabucco,* offering to sing the role of Abigaille before she had heard a note of it, who persuaded the leading baritone of La Scala to assume the title role, and who then persuaded Merelli to produce the work. Strepponi's instincts about *Nabucco* had been absolutely sound. The work was so popular that it broke the house record by being given at La Scala fifty-seven times in one season.

What a splendid friend she was to the inexperienced young man! In age she was two years younger than Verdi, but in hard-headed theatrical

The gateway to Sant'Agata, Verdi's retreat from the world for over half a century. In 1848 he bought a tract of farmland in Emilia, building a villa with hard-earned royalties. Around the home is a wooded park, with shady gravel walkways, grottos and a pond, where swans peacefully glide to this day

and worldly experience she was years older. Strepponi was a gold mine of practical advice in matters that baffled the former church organist. How much should he charge Merelli for a new opera requested by the impresario? Something reasonably profitable, she suggested, but something not impossibly high. How about the same fee Bellini had received ten years before for *Norma*? Everyone was happy about the idea, and *I Lombardi* was begun.

Yet even as she watched the career of her new friend grow and flourish, Strepponi had to face the cruel truth that her own career was coming to a close. Doctors who examined her shortly after the premiere of *Nabucco* reported that "her once beautiful and sonorous voice was found—also by the public—to be weak, veiled and insufficient, even when emitted with extraordinary effort." They pronounced that Signora Strepponi was "affected with such laryngo-tracheal inflammation as will lead to consumption unless she at once ceases to exercise her profession and submits herself to careful treatment and an uninterruptedly tranquil way of life." Medically unsound as this conclusion might have been, it does give us a dismal picture of poor Strepponi's vocal problems.

What had happened to cut short a career as brilliant and musically sound as Strepponi's when the singer was only twenty-six years old and had been singing in public for little more than seven years? We have no way of knowing for sure, but it seems almost certain that Strepponi was the victim of the brutal over-working of voices so common in the Bellini-Donizetti-early-Verdi era. It was not unusual for a singer to take on the taxing roles five times a week. Frank Walker cites the incident of Strepponi, having been ill one week, being required to sing six times the next in order to "make up" the loss.

Strepponi's tendency to overwork and to accept roles not suited to her voice was rooted in hard necessity. She had to support her mother and the young brothers and sisters left fatherless in 1842. There were also her own two children, born out of wedlock to one of her regular tenors, Napoleone Moriani. These small encumbrances to her career were the result of an infatuation for the romantic and wholly irresponsible tenor in whose company the starry-eyed young soprano was forced by her profession to spend much time while traveling from opera house to opera house.

With her Italian operatic career drawing to a close, Giuseppina made a bold move. She went to Paris to seek her fortune in a center of musical sophistication which would appreciate an artist of her caliber. "La Strepponi," a Parisian journal reported shortly after her arrival, "is known in Italy not only as a great singer, but still more as a woman of much wit and spirit. She has always been greatly sought after by the world of the nobility, who, after having applauded her on the stage, loved to applaud and admire her in their most brilliant gatherings." Strepponi sang a number of concerts, gave singing lessons to ladies ("designed for the finishing of amateurs or artists who wish to acquire complete knowledge of the art") and flourished in Paris. And here, in the spring of 1847, her path once more crossed that of Giuseppe Verdi.

Exactly how and when did the two old friends become lovers and start living together? Verdi scholars have searched out, examined and weighed every shred of evidence in an effort to sort fact from fiction. Accounts and opinions vary. What matters is that Verdi and his lovely Peppina did find each other again, did fall in love and begin a new life, a life together that would last fifty years, until Peppina's death in 1897.

For practical and political reasons the lovers remained in Paris, where Verdi worked on *Il Corsaro,* one of his distinctly minor achievements. Verdi and Strepponi, united by their ardent patriotism as well as their love, were tremendously stirred by the news that reached Paris about events at home. The pandemic revolutionary activity of 1848 naturally made itself felt strongly in Italy. In March open rebellion flared in Milan, and for five days a battle raged between the Milanese and the Austrian oppressors.

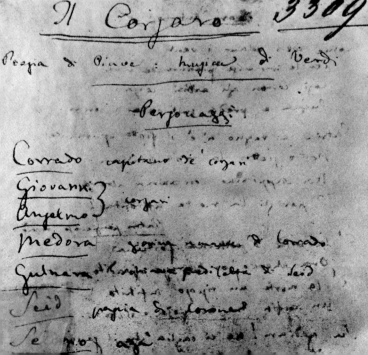

GRAN TEATRO DI TRIESTE
Per la sera di Mercoldì 25 Ottobre 1848
PARI N.° 26.

Prima Rappresentazione
DELLA NUOVISSIMA OPERA
IN TRE ATTI:
Il Corsaro
Parole di Fr. M. Piave. - Musica del Maestro G. Verdi
non mai esposta in altri Teatri.

PERSONAGGI

CORRADO, Capitano de' Corsari	Fraschini Gaetano
GIOVANNI, Corsaro	Volpini Giovanni
MEDORA, amante di Corrado	Rapazzini Carolina
GULNARA, Schiava di Seid	Barbieri-Nini Marianna
SEID, Pacia di Corone	De Bassini Achille
SELIMO, Agà	Petrovich Giovanni
FUNUCO, nero	Cucchiari Francesco
Uno SCHIAVO	Albanassich Stefano

Cori e Comparse
Corsari - Guardie - Turchi - Schiavi - Odalische.

Lo Spettacolo incomincierà alle ore 7 1/2 precise.

NB. - I Signori Abbonati riceveranno i Libretti al Bigoncio.

"Imagine whether I wished to remain in Paris, hearing of a revolution at Milan!" Verdi wrote to Piave. "I left as soon as I heard the news but was only able to see the stupendous barricades. Honor to these brave men! Honor to all Italy, which at this moment is truly great! The hour has sounded—be convinced of it—for her liberation. It is the people that wills it, and when the people wills there is no absolute power that can resist. . . . You talk of music to me! What are you thinking of? . . . There is, and should be, only one kind of music pleasing to the ears of the Italians of 1848—the music of the guns! I would not write a note for all the gold in the world: I should feel immense remorse for using up music paper, which is so good to make cartridges with."

Il Corsaro *was the second of two operas Verdi drew from the works of Lord Byron (the first:* I Due Foscari). *A romantic yarn about pirates and Turks, the opera failed to sustain his interest, and he did not even attend the world premiere at the Teatro Grande of Trieste in 1848. A successful revival of* Il Corsaro *was staged at the Teatro la Fenice of Venice in 1971 by director Alberto Fassini and designer Pier Luigi Pizzi. Shown here, their harem scene (top left) and Katia Ricciarelli as Medora (right). At bottom left are the first page of Piave's libretto and the world premiere playbill*

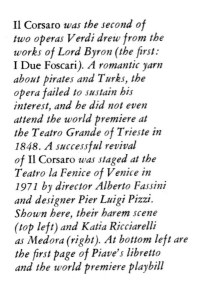

But music paper in the hands of Verdi could be far more explosive than cartridges. He returned to Paris and Peppina, but his mind was seething with political fervor. His librettist Cammarano had once suggested as an opera subject the defeat of Barbarossa, the Holy Roman emperor, by the Italians of the Lombard League. The opera Cammarano had in mind might be called *La Battaglia di Legnano,* and might be set in 1176, but Italy and all the world would know what it was really about!

And so the opera was written. It is easy to imagine the frenzy with which Rome greeted its premiere at that particular moment in history. Pope Piux IX had fled the city; Garibaldi and Mazzini had entered it, to help celebrate a republican victory at the polls; the audience at every performance of *La Battaglia* went clean out of its mind as early as the opening chorus, which proclaimed, "Long live Italy! A sacred pact binds

In La Battaglia di Legnano, *Verdi boldly protested Austrian domination of Italy. The story of the Lombard League's defeat of Barbarossa in 1176, it premiered at the Teatro Argentina in 1849, two weeks after Rome declared herself a republic. In 1961, La Scala, Milan, unearthed this militant epic for Franco Corelli (right)*

all her sons!'' The entire last act had to be encored at every performance. Needless to say, the frenzied public accolades heaped on *La Battaglia di Legnano* were based more on national aspiration than on sound musical judgment.

Obviously, since Italian unification was still some years away, the mighty hopes of those days were soon dead. Nothing worked out according to promise. The Austrians marched back into Milan. Garibaldi retreated. The French entered Rome. "Don't let us talk of Rome!'' wrote Verdi, more than ever a hero of the city. "What good would it do? Force still rules the world. And justice? What use is it against bayonets? All we can do is weep over our wrongs and curse the authors of so many misfortunes."

Verdi's long sojourn in Paris was coming to an end. He was there

just long enough to begin *Luisa Miller* (he would finish it in Busseto). When the lovers returned to Italy, Peppina stayed a few days in Florence to make arrangements for the schooling of her son. Finally, in September 1849, Verdi and Strepponi took the step that called upon all their innate dignity, inner resources and courage, even though they had known all along that it was coming.

Considering the supersonic speed with which rumor spreads—particularly scandalous rumor originating in a small Italian town of the mid-nineteenth century—it must have taken the mere wink of an eye for the entire population of Busseto and suburbs to hear the news that their own Maestro Giuseppe Verdi, pride and delight of the community, had moved back into his home, the Palazzo Dordoni, and that a strange woman had moved in with him . . . a woman of the theater . . . a woman ("Orrore!") to whom he was not married.

Outrage in Busseto. Indignation in the surrounding villages. It is easy to imagine the slights and insults, subtle and unsubtle, to which poor Peppina was subjected. Proximity to the center of town was one factor in the snub campaign. In 1851 the lovers went to live in Verdi's farmhouse at Sant'Agata, a place of peace and solitude two miles from Busseto.

Luisa Miller, introduced in Naples in 1849, brought Verdi into his rich middle period, where introspective personal feelings gained the dominant voice. The plot, drawn from a Schiller play, concerns an innocent peasant maid undone by perfidious noblemen, a popular theme during the nineteenth century. A new production of Luisa Miller *was staged at the Metropolitan Opera in 1968 with rich décor by Attilio Colonnello. Shown here are Mignon Dunn as Federica (far left) and Montserrat Caballé as the expiring Luisa, attended by Sherrill Milnes as her father, Miller, and Richard Tucker as her beloved, Rodolfo*

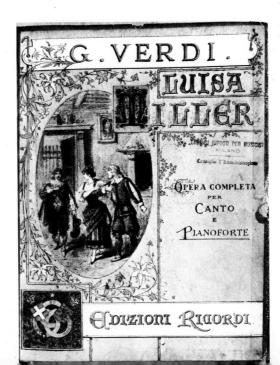

Away from the palpable disapproval of the local gentry, life became simpler and markedly more agreeable. Verdi became an enthusiastic gardener and farmer. He planted trees—a new tree invariably marked the premiere of each new work. He raised cattle. He grew corn and wine-producing grapes. The people of Busseto, although they had claimed to be scandalized by the sight of the sinful couple, managed to be even more outraged at the idea that the two were now living peacefully out of sight in the country.

Verdi's usual reticence on the subject of his life with Peppina was broken once, in a remarkable letter to Antonio Barezzi. It is a letter, he makes clear, written not in anger but with the greatest respect and affection for the man he called his second father; but it reveals like no other word he has left us the depth of his feeling about Giuseppina's position.

"I don't believe that of your own accord," he wrote, "you would have written me a letter which you know was bound to distress me. But you live in a town where people have the bad habit of prying into other people's affairs and disapproving of everything that does not conform to their own ideas. It is my custom never to interfere, unless I am asked, in other people's business, and I expect others not to interfere in mine. I have the right to expect in my own country the liberty of action that is respected even in less civilized places. Judge for yourself. . . . What harm is there if I live in isolation? If I choose not to pay calls to titled people? If I take no part in the festivities and rejoicings of others? If I administer my farmlands because I like to do so, and because it amuses me? I ask again: What harm is there in this? In any case, no one is the worse for it. . . .

"There, I've laid bare to you my opinions, my actions, my wishes, my public life I would almost say, and since we are by way of making revelations, I have no objection to raising the curtain that veils the mysteries contained within four walls and telling you about my private life. I have nothing to hide. In my house there lives a lady, free, independent, a lover like myself of solitude, possessing a fortune that shelters her from all need. Neither I nor she owes to anyone at all an account of our actions. On the other hand, who knows what relationship exists between us? What affairs? What ties? What claims I have on her, and she on me? Who knows whether she is or is not my wife? And if she is, who knows what the particular reasons are for not making the fact public? Who knows whether that is a good thing or a bad one? Why should it not be a good thing?

A Protestant minister whose wife has committed adultery seems an unlikely plot for an Italian opera, but Verdi, in quest of human drama, utilized such a story in Stiffelio, *first heard at Trieste's Teatro Grande in 1850. Seven years later in Rimini, Verdi brought forth a much revised version,* Aroldo

And even if it is a bad thing, who has the right to ostracize us? I will say this, however: in my house she is entitled to as much respect as myself—more, even; and no one is allowed to forget that on any account. And finally she has every right, both on account of her conduct and her character, to the consideration she never fails to show to others."

Whatever ill-feeling and misunderstanding had prompted this letter, the sense of father-son affection between Verdi and Barezzi was soon stronger than ever, and the good old man's affection reached out to embrace Peppina as warmly. In letters to him she signed herself "your most affectionate quasi-daughter."

Why in fact did Verdi, with his great sensitivity to Peppina's feelings, delay so long in legalizing the marriage that already existed so solidly in their hearts? Again we have nothing to rely upon but scholarly conjecture, and there are areas in human lives, even great lives that eventually belong to the world, which are forever inaccessible to the probing of posterity. It seems likely that it was Peppina herself who hung back, feeling herself unworthy of marriage to Verdi. (Who can fathom a passionate, conflicting Italian conscience like Peppina's?) Perhaps the delay had something to do with Peppina's children by Moriani, poor shadowy figures who hover silently on the edge of her recorded history. Of Peppina's all-encompassing love for Verdi there has never been any question, in spite of the stress and strain inevitable when one is united with a genius.

We have a magnificent set of letters written by Peppina when Verdi was away from her and Sant'Agata. One of these, dating from 1860, gives us an unforgettable picture of her love. "Perhaps when this letter arrives," it reads in part, "you will be at Turin, if as you intend you decide definitely to see Cavour and Sir James. What a thing it is to have genius! One goes to pay calls on ministers of state and ambassadors, just as I go to see Giovanna. And yet what obliges the world to take off its hat to you is the quality of which I never think, or hardly ever.

"I swear to you, and you won't have difficulty believing it, that many times I am quite surprised you know anything about music! However divine that art, and however worthy your genius of the art you profess, the talisman that fascinates me and that I adore in you is your character, your heart, your indulgence for the mistakes of others while you are so severe with yourself, your charity, full of modesty and mystery, your proud independence and your boyish simplicity—qualities proper to that nature of yours which has been able to conserve a primal virginity of ideas and sentiments in the midst of the human *cloaca*! My Verdi, I am not worthy of you, and the love you bear me is charity, balsam, to a heart sometimes very sad beneath the appearances of cheerfulness. Continue to love me; love me also after death, so that I may present myself to Divine Providence rich with your love and your prayers, O my Redeemer!"

This letter was written a year after the two lovers were married. Another area of mystery and conjecture enters the story: if this curious wedding ceremony had been staged in an opera instead of in life, it would certainly have been one by Cimarosa or Rossini, not by Verdi! There are few details available. On August 29, 1859, after twelve years of life together, Verdi and Peppina were married in a completely private ceremony at Collonges-sous-Salève, a little town in Savoy not far from the Italian border.

Arrangements for the marriage were made by Verdi's friend the Abbé Mermillod, rector of the Church of Notre Dame in Geneva. The wedding party, consisting of bride, groom and Abbé, drove in a cab from Geneva to Collonges-sous-Salève, told the local priest to take a walk outside, went through the ceremony with the cab driver and the local bellringer as witnesses—and drove off again. Verdi mentions the event once, never again making reference to it in any of his later correspondence. But however odd the circumstances, Peppina was now Signora Verdi in name as well as fact.

V

THE CENSORS AND RIGOLETTO

IN the year 1850, Verdi was just about to enter upon those great days in his creative life on which his enduring reputation would be built. Casting about for a subject that would provide a new opera for the coming season, he mulled over the ideas that would eventually lead to *Rigoletto* and *Il Trovatore*. He even sketched a synopsis for the opera he would never write: *King Lear*. And from this multiplicity of fruitful ideas what opera finally emerged? *Stiffelio*! The whole thing was Piave's idea. What ever possessed Verdi to accept the suggestion and actually set a story so basically un-Verdian? Everyone is entitled to an occasional error in judgment, but this tale of a Protestant minister whose wife commits adultery was simply not the stuff of which great Verdi operas are made. (Seven years later the opera was redone as

Verdi reached a new plane of expression with Rigoletto, *adapted for Venice in 1851 from Victor Hugo's* Le Roi s'Amuse. *The Metropolitan Opera's historic 1972 revival starred Joan Sutherland (Gilda), Sherrill Milnes (Rigoletto), Luciano Pavarotti (Duke of Mantua) and Batyah Godfrey (Maddalena), all shown at left*

Aroldo, with the Swiss pastor inversely reincarnated as an English crusader. It didn't help.)

The Italian Catholic censors were greatly upset by the idea of a married clergyman whose unfaithful wife confesses her sin to him. The clear implication that it is a Christian virtue to forgive marital infidelity must also have seemed a strange, foreign idea. In any case *Stiffelio* had to go through considerable "expurgation" before it reached the stage.

If Verdi had endured trials by censor in the past, they were nothing compared to what hit him as he and Piave prepared for the premiere of *Rigoletto,* which was to open at La Fenice on March 11, 1851. Less than a year earlier, while keeping in the back of his mind the play that would soon become *Il Trovatore,* Verdi had written to Piave: "I have in mind another subject," he started out, "which, if the police would allow it, is one of the greatest creations of the modern theater. . . . It includes a character who is one of the greatest creations that the theater of all nations and all times can boast. The story is *Le Roi s'Amuse,* and the character I mean is Triboulet, a creation worthy of Shakespeare."

There was good reason for Verdi to suggest that the police or some other censor might take a dim view of making an opera out of Victor Hugo's play. After all, the play lasted exactly one night when it opened in Paris on November 22, 1832. The next day it was closed on grounds of immorality, and was not seen again in Paris for fifty years. In spite of that history, Piave persuaded Verdi that the Austrian censors would have no objection to the play once it had become a Verdi-Piave opera. Imagine their shock when Verdi heard from the management of the Fenice, just three months before the opera was due to open, that the authorities did indeed object, and vehemently. What's more, they concluded their objections by saying they did not care to discuss the matter any further. The management had received this letter from the Imperial Director of Theaters:

Rigoletto remains the earliest Verdi work in the standard repertory. Among its musical treasures is the opera's split-action quartet, (top right), in which the dissolute Duke courts Maddalena while the suffering Gilda and Rigoletto watch. A celebrated Jester and Gilda of the 1930s were Giuseppe De Luca and Lily Pons (right)

RIGOLETTO
MELODRAMMA DI F. M. PIAVE MUSICA DEL MAESTRO
G. VERDI

Il più caro de suoi amici, l'egregio toscato

ANTONIO VASSELLI

in pegno di gratissimo cuore questa edizione consacra
GIOVANNI RICORDI

MILANO

"His Excellency the Military Governor Chevalier Gorzkowski in his respected dispatch of the 26th instant, N. 731, directs me to communicate to you his profound regret that the poet Piave and the celebrated maestro Verdi should not have chosen a more worthy vehicle to display their talents than the revolting immorality and obscene triviality of the libretto of *La Maledizione,* submitted to us for intended performance at the Teatro Fenice.

"His above mentioned Excellency has decided that the performance shall be absolutely forbidden, and wishes me at the same time to request you not to make further inquiries in this matter. I am returning the manuscript sent to me with your accompanying letter of the 20th instant. N. 18."

Paying no attention to the imperial suggestion "not to make further inquiries," Verdi quickly found out that the censors did not like a story in which a king behaved in a profligate manner and went unpunished and untroubled in conscience, in which a curse was a central motivating force in the drama, and in which certain incidents seemed obscene and immoral.

Piave, always ready to play Milquetoast, soon sent Verdi a revised libretto, in which he had made the changes required by the censors. But Verdi was in a fighting mood and had no intention of giving in.

"I have taken very little time to examine the new libretto," he wrote to Carlo Marzari, the director of La Fenice, on December 14, 1850. "But I have seen enough to know that in this form its lacks character and meaning, and the dramatic points have all been nullified. If it was necessary to change the names of the characters, then the place should have been changed as well so that [the king] could be made into a duke or prince of another country, for instance a Pier Luigi Farnese or someone else; or else the action should have been changed back to the period before Louis XI, when France was not a united kingdom, and he could have been a Duke of Burgundy or Normandy, etc., etc., in any case an absolute ruler. In the fifth scene of Act I, all those courtiers raging against Triboletto do not make any sense. The old man's curse, so terrifying and sublime in the original, becomes ridiculous here, because the motivation for the curse is not so important any more and because this is no longer a subject speaking so daringly to his king. Without this malediction what purpose, what point is left to the drama? The duke becomes a cipher, but it is essential that he be a libertine. Otherwise there is no reason for Triboletto's fear that his daughter will leave her hiding place, and the entire drama is impossible. Why should the duke go, in the last act, to a remote tavern, alone, unless he has had an invitation to a rendezvous?"

As Verdi continues, his anger at the senseless objections mounts. "I don't understand why the sack was taken out!" he storms. "What difference did the sack make to the police? Are they afraid of its effect? But let me ask this: why do they think they know more about it than I do? Who can be sure? Who can say this will work and that will not? We had the same problem with the horn in *Ernani*. But did anyone laugh at that horn? If we have no sack it is improbable that Triboletto would talk to the body for half an hour without a flash of lightning revealing it to be his daughter's.

"Finally I note that Triboletto is not to be ugly or a hunchback. Why? A singing hunchback? Why not? Will it be effective? I don't know. But if I don't know, neither does the person who proposed these changes. In my view the idea of this character, outwardly ridiculous and deformed, inwardly filled with passion and love, is superb. It was precisely because of these original and characteristic traits that I chose the subject, and if they are cut out I will be unable to write the music. If I am told that my music will do just as well for this drama as for the other, I must answer that I simply do not understand such reasoning, and I state frankly that whether my music is good or bad, I never write at random and I

always try to give my music a distinct character. In short," Verdi concluded, "what was an original and powerful play has been turned into
something very ordinary and uninteresting. I very much regret that the
Board of Directors has not answered my last letter. I can only repeat what
I said in it, that my artistic conscience will not permit me to set this
libretto to music."

Within two weeks from the date of Verdi's letter, a compromise had
been reached in which changes acceptable to Verdi were agreed upon.
Marzari sent his secretary, Guglielmo Brenna, to Busseto, where together
with the composer and the librettist he drew up an official document of
agreement. Signed at Verdi's home on December 30, it stipulated that
the sack could remain in the final scene, that the king or duke would go
to the tavern as the result of a pretended invitation brought to him by
the jester, and among other things that the name of the jester would be
changed from Triboletto to Rigoletto. Not only was Verdi satisfied, but
when the opera became an instant success he enjoyed pointing out that
most of the situations in Hugo's play had been left without change. Hugo
himself was understandably irritated that the opera could be seen and
heard in Paris while his play was still under official ban. The Parisians
raved over it so vociferously that the first season it reached their city it
was performed there more than a hundred times. When Hugo finally
heard it, he was forced to confess his admiration for it. After the famous
quartet, he said what many playwrights must often have thought when
they hear opera's great ensembles: "If I could only make four characters
in my plays speak at the same time, and have the audience grasp the words
and sentiments, I would obtain the very same effect."

Seldom had censors made a more devastating frontal attack on a
proposed opera and caused so little basic change in the drama. Verdi was
learning the subtleties of how and when to fight back.

The Metropolitan Opera has played Rigoletto *nearly 400 times, a
production designed by Eugene Berman in 1951 serving for a quarter
of a century. Shown here are his Act I, the Duke's court (top left),
Leonard Warren as Rigoletto (bottom far left) and the Act III
duet of Gilda and her father, Renata Scotto and Cornell MacNeil*

VI

TRIUMPHS AND
A TEMPORARY SETBACK

FOR those who like to divide Verdi's operas into early, middle and late, *Rigoletto* is the clear marker with which the middle period begins. From this point on there are no significant weak moments. All the time he was at work on *Rigoletto,* Verdi's mind was filled with another play that had, to his way of thinking, everything. By the Spanish playwright Gutiérrez, it was called *El Trovador.* Its action was of the blood-and-guts variety Verdi associated with Cammarano, the man who had written his librettos for *Alzira, La Battaglia di Legnano* and *Luisa Miller.* But when Verdi received Cammarano's first outline for the new opera, he wrote back. "I have read your sketch," he began. "As a gifted and most exceptional man, you will not be offended if I humbly take the liberty of saying it would be better to give up this subject if we

Il Trovatore *was the last Verdi opera conceived in the bel canto style brought to perfection by Bellini, Rossini and Donizetti. At the Metropolitan Opera in 1973, two bel canto stylists took leading roles—Montserrat Caballé as the lady Leonora (far left) and Fiorenza Cossotto as Azucena (left)*

cannot manage to retain all the boldness and novelty of the Spanish play."
Then, as he often did, Verdi sent along an outline indicating his own
ideas. His letter was dated April 9, 1851. Three months later, without
warning and after finishing two and a half acts of *Il Trovatore*, Cammarano died.

Verdi was shocked. "I was thunderstruck by the sad news of Cammarano," he wrote a friend. "I can't describe the depth of my sorrow.
I read of his death not in a letter from a friend but in a stupid journal.
You loved him as much as I did, and will understand the feelings I cannot
find words for. Poor Cammarano. What a loss." It was with his usual
generosity that Verdi sent the poet's widow 600 ducats, a hundred over
the agreed-upon figure.

Cammarano's death left Verdi, in July, without a completed libretto
for an opera promised to the Apollo Theater in Rome the following
January. To finish the book he hired a young poet named Bardare, who
did a decent job with the materials he was given. There are those who
claim that the story of this opera is so hopelessly confused and confusing
there is no point in worrying about it. (Other Verdi-lovers insist that
Piave's book for *Simon Boccanegra* is at least as puzzling as the Camma-
rano-Bardare rendering of Gutiérrez' play.) The Roman audience that
first heard *Il Trovatore* ate it up. The day after the premiere the *Musical
Gazette* said, "The public listened to each number in religious silence,
breaking out into applause at every interval." As in the case of *La Battaglia
di Legnano,* the entire last act had to be repeated.

In less than a decade from that first night, Verdi was writing from
London to his friend Count Opprandino Arrivabene. He had gone to
the British capital to attend the International Exhibition, for which he
had written only the rather inconsequential *Hymn of the Nations.* "As for
Italy," he wrote the count, "her music needs no performing at the exhibition. It gets performed here every evening at two theaters, and not only
here but everywhere. . . . Never before at any time have there been so

many Italian opera houses, never have publishers of every country printed and sold so much Italian music; and there isn't a corner of this earth where there's a theater and a couple of instruments and no Italian opera being sung. If you should ever go to the Indies or to the interior of Africa, you'll hear *Il Trovatore*."

Verdi had chosen Rome's Apollo Theater for the premiere of his newest opera because the singers offered to him there best suited his requirements. As his reputation grew, so did his power to pick and choose among the offers that besieged him. Yet the opera that followed *Il Trovatore* failed in its first season, a failure due at least in part to the fact that Verdi could not fully exercise this option. The opera was *La Traviata,* third in the triumvirate of Verdi greats that occupy a special niche among all his operas: *Rigoletto, Il Trovatore, La Traviata*. It was heard for the first time in La Fenice in Venice, exactly forty-six days after the huge success of *Il Trovatore* in Rome. Never before or again were two operas by Verdi given their first performances so close together. But the closeness of the dates had nothing to do with the disaster that struck the night of that first *Traviata.*

"Unfortunately I have to send you sad news," Verdi wrote to Giulio Ricordi the morning after the opening. "I can't conceal the truth from you. *Traviata* was a fiasco. Don't try to work out the reason, that's just the way it is."

To his old friend Muzio he wrote, "Dear Emmanuele: *Traviata* last night—a fiasco. Was it my fault or the singers'? Time will tell."

His most prophetic note was sounded in the letter he sent to Angelo Mariani: "*La Traviata* was a great fiasco and, what is worse, they laughed. Still, what can I say? I am not upset by it. Am I wrong or are they? I myself believe that the last word on *La Traviata* was not heard last night. They will hear it again—and we shall see! Meanwhile, dear Mariani, note the fiasco."

"Was it my fault or the singers'?" Verdi asked Muzio. He had not

held the veto power over the principals at La Fenice, and he had been worried about them weeks before the premiere. The baritone, Varesi, had sung the first Macbeth and had carried off well the heavy responsibilities of Rigoletto in the stunning premiere of that opera. But the elder Germont in *Traviata* is a very different kind of character from the powerhouse baritones Varesi had sung previously, and he had failed to make a strong impression.

It is not, however, the baritone or the tenor that makes or breaks a *Traviata*. It is, at least among the principals, the soprano. And the soprano at La Fenice the night they opened *Traviata* was bound for trouble no matter how she sang. Fanny Salvini-Donatelli, the first woman to sing the frail Violetta, was no sylph. It would be euphemistic to refer to her as statuesque. She was, in a word, fat. Some reports have weighed her in at over 300 pounds. Did Verdi say, "They laughed"? No wonder. What else could the Venetians do at the sight of her steady decline from what was called in those days the "galloping consumption"? Even today's sometimes more tolerant audiences have difficulty in watching an Aida who weighs well over that figure being knocked to the floor by an Amonasro half her size.

And so, like its heroine, *Traviata* went into a decline after the season's ten performances. Verdi then moved promptly. He forbade any further productions unless he could take personal charge of them. For more than a year the opera was not heard. Then it returned—again in Venice, but this time at the Teatro San Benedetto, with Piave in charge of the direction.

Verdi took special pleasure in pointing out that the opera, of whose eventual worth he had never had a serious doubt, was now a success, and with the same people in the same city listening to the same opera they had not so long ago derided.

If the time between the premieres of *Il Trovatore* and *La Traviata*

Rescue scenes à la Trovatore: *at top left, Count di Luna (Sherrill Milnes) foiled by Manrico (Placido Domingo), who saves Leonora (Leontyne Price) from his clutches at bottom left, King Victor Emmanuel, garbed as Manrico, embraces Lady Italy. Also shown, Claudia Muzio as Leonora and Carlo Bergonzi as Manrico*

was the shortest in the history of Verdi operas, that which elapsed between the opening of *La Traviata* and its successor was one of the longer intervals until late in his career. Not even after the death of his two children and his wife had there been so long a period between premieres. But the new opera was being written on commission from the Paris Opera for the Great Exhibition of 1855, and it was giving Verdi problems he did not enjoy.

"A work for the Opéra is enough to stun a bull!" he wrote to a friend. "Five hours of music. Phew!" The proportions of *Les Vêpres Siciliennes*, the name under which it was unveiled in Paris in June of the year of the exposition, were not Verdi's only problems in working at what quickly became uncongenial to him. He could adapt his music to the heroic requirements beloved in French opera since the days of Lully and Rameau. The large spectacle was as welcome to the composer of *Nabucco* and *La Battaglia di Legnano* as it was to Meyerbeer and Halévy, and

Violetta in La Traviata *tests the singing and acting abilities of a soprano to the limit. Among the most memorable interpreters of this most touching Verdi heroine at the Metropolitan Opera are Lucrezia Bori (during the 1920s and '30s), Licia Albanese (1940s, '50s, '60s) and Maria Callas (1958), all shown below*

before he was through Verdi would outdo them all with what quickly became the world's favorite "spectacle" opera. Verdi's chief problem as he rehearsed the new opera was that its librettist, the famous Eugène Scribe, had included some offensive material in the libretto as well as some Verdi thought impossibly conventional and routine. Though the big-name writer had assured Verdi he would change the most objectionable of these, he never did so.

Scribe was twenty-two years older than Verdi. He had provided librettos for some of the most famous operas of Meyerbeer, Bellini, Donizetti, Halévy, Rossini and dozens more. His huge output was possible thanks to the number of hack writers he hired to work in one of the busiest writing factories in Paris (the other was run by Dumas); Charles Duveyrier was the man Scribe assigned to work on the book of *Les Vêpres Siciliennes*. This was hardly the treatment to which Verdi was accustomed, nor did the Scribe-Duveyrier system give the composer any chance for the

Less than a success at its world premiere in Venice in 1853,
La Traviata *has since become a beloved classic. Shown below at the Metropolitan Opera are Robert Merrill and Anna Moffo in the Act II confrontation of Germont and Violetta and the company's 1976* Lady of the Camelias, *Beverly Sills*

exchange of ideas he had always enjoyed. At last, after enduring slighting remarks from the singers during rehearsals, Verdi was fed up.

"It is possible there are people who do not think my music worthy of the Opéra," he wrote to its director. "It is possible there are others who think their roles unworthy of their talents. It is possible that I, for my part, find the performance and the style of singing other than I would have wished! In short it seems to me, unless I am strangely mistaken, that we are not at one in our way of feeling and interpreting the music, and without perfect accord there can be no possible success."

Perhaps Verdi's strong words, and his open suggestion that he withdraw from the entire project, had some effect. In any case, six months later, on June 13, 1855, *Les Vêpres Siciliennes* was a huge hit with public and press alike. It quickly ran up a total of fifty performances the first season. Years later, when Verdi saw the premiere of *Le Duc d'Albe* by Donizetti, an opera with a Scribe libretto, a bright light went on in his head. "Now I understand," he wrote, remembering his problems with the Scribe-Duveyrier libretto. "I truly believe that *I Vespri* was taken from *Il Duca d'Alba!*"

After the success of *Les Vêpres Siciliennes* in Paris, Verdi must have felt a special pleasure in returning to Italy, where he soon began work on another Piave text for an opera to be given at La Fenice in the spring of 1857. A year before the new opera, however, Verdi took the greatest delight in conducting a revival of *Traviata* in the very theater where three years earlier it had been a dismal failure. This time the Fenice audience had trouble expressing its enthusiasm loudly enough. It was as if it wanted to atone for the short-sightedness on the part of that earlier audience. Verdi and La Fenice were again a winning combination. But not for long.

On March 12, 1857, *Simon Boccanegra* had its first hearing, and again La Fenice brought disaster, though Verdi seemed far less disturbed by it than he had been at the time of the *Traviata* failure. In a note to the

Paris commissioned Les Vêpres Siciliennes, *an epic in Meyerbeer style about a thirteenth-century Sicilian massacre of the French, first staged in 1855. Shown at left in the Metropolitan Opera's 1974 staging are Montserrat Caballé as Elena, Sherrill Milnes as Monforte and Nicolai Gedda as his son, Arrigo*

Countess Maffei he linked the two: "*Boccanegra* was almost a greater fiasco in Venice than *Traviata,*" he wrote. "I thought I had done something fairly good, but now it seems I was mistaken." As it turned out twenty-three years later, when he agreed with Giulio Ricordi that a revision of *Boccanegra* was a good idea, Verdi indicated he knew what the score's weak points were.

"The score as it stands is impossible. It is too sad, too desolate . . . the whole of the second act must be revised and given more relief," he said, putting his finger on precisely those places that became, in the revision, greatly strengthened. He had known from the beginning that Piave was not producing a strong libretto. He had even asked a friend, Giuseppe Montanelli, to rewrite some scenes. But it would take a stronger hand than Montanelli's to fix things properly.

Meanwhile, Verdi was again heading into censorship difficulties. There had been a hint of these while *Boccanegra* was in the works, but Verdi had simply said he would make no changes and the matter was not pursued by the authorities. Now, however, he had set his sights on, of all things, a libretto by Scribe. It was to bring him into a conflict with the censors that only the *Rigoletto* brouhaha topped. The libretto was based on a historical event, the assassination in 1792 of King Gustav III of Sweden. To shape a libretto for him out of the one Scribe or one of his flunkies had written for Auber's *Gustave III,* Verdi turned for the first and only time to Antonio Somma. He knew, even before Somma got to work, that the police would be breathing down his neck once they heard he wanted to write an opera about a king murdered onstage. But he had not dreamed that the censors in Naples, with whom he had contracted for the opera, would not permit the opera to be given there regardless of any changes in locale or period or royal rank.

The censors had some reason on their side: Europe in 1859 was not all peace and quiet, politically speaking. The year before, some anarchist

Verdi wrote Simon Boccanegra *for Venice, where he was caricatured during rehearsals by Melchiorre Delfico (bottom left). First given in 1857, the work was heavily revised some two decades later. Shown at left at the Metropolitan Opera are Cornell MacNeil (Boccanegra), Rita Orlandi Malaspina (Maria), Richard Tucker (Gabriele)*

had thrown a bomb under the carriage that was carrying Napoleon III to the Opéra. Such an open threat against the life of a king was more than enough for the Neapolitan censor to scotch the whole project. Yet here were Verdi and Somma proposing a finale in which a king is murdered before everyone's eyes! Whether the regicide was to be by stabbing or gunshot must have seemed immaterial to the censor.

Perhaps the censor might have let them proceed had Verdi been willing to make these changes, the request for which Verdi told Somma he had received:

1) Change the hero into an ordinary gentleman—no king; 2) Change the wife into a sister! 3) Change the fortune-telling scene, placing it in a time when "people believed in such things"; 4) No ball! 5) Any murder had to be offstage; 6) Omit the name-drawing scene. "And, and, and!!" Verdi wrote to Somma. "As you can imagine, these changes are out of the question, so no more opera. So the subscribers won't pay the last two installments, so the government will withdraw the subsidy, so the directors will sue everyone, and already threaten me with damages of 50,000 ducats. What the hell!"

Rescue came from the most unlikely source: the Apollo Theater in Rome sent word that it would produce the new opera, to be called *Un Ballo in Maschera,* provided the papal censor had no objections and assuming that Verdi could make peace with the Naples theater. Apparently the murder of a king did not upset the papal censor at that moment, just as

long as no one tried it on a pope! The censor did ask for one small adjustment, thereby winning for himself a permanent if peculiar place in operatic annals. To him we owe one of the oddest settings in all Verdiana: pre-Revolutionary Boston.

So those strange operatic conspirators Sam and Tom were hatched, King Gustav became Riccardo, Governor of Boston, and Amelia goes to fetch her magic herb at midnight underneath a gallows located somewhere near Dedham.

Somma, new to all this business, was, Verdi wrote a friend about the whole mess, "nauseated." Verdi took a more philosophical view: "From Rome I have received the variants for *Ballo in Maschera*. Somma . . . is nauseated by them (the word is not polite), and I am more than he. But what could I have done? Did he want me to protest and start a lawsuit like last year? . . . In the theater, of course, one has to make sacrifices, and it's useless for anyone who hasn't the courage to do this to expose himself to this severe trial."

And so it came about that in Rome on that February night in 1859 *Ballo* created not only a brilliant reception for its composer but brought out shouts of "Viva Verdi!"—a rallying cry in the outburst of patriotism that was again sweeping over Italy. Before the year was over, Verdi would be elected to represent Busseto in the assembly at Parma. And on the 29th of August in the same year he would at last marry Giuseppina in that peculiar ceremony in Collonges.

UN BALLO IN MASCHERA

Melodramma in tre atti

MUSICA DI

GIUSEPPE VERDI

DA RAPPRESENTARSI

AL TEATRO APOLLO IN ROMA

il Carnevale 1859

MILANO

DALL' I. R. STABILIMENTO NAZIONALE PRIVILEGIATO DI

TITO DI GIO. RICORDI

Un Ballo in Maschera *gave Verdi problems with the censors, who objected to the subject of regicide. Thus, at the Rome premiere in 1859, Verdi made the hero a governor, not a king. At left at the Metropolitan Opera are Placido Domingo as Riccardo and Reri Grist as Oscar*

VII

VIVA VERDI!

IN January 1859, Vittorio Emmanuele assured the Italian people that he was fully aware of their sufferings. In February V-E-R-D-I and Vittorio Emmanuele Re d'Italia became a patriotic synonym. In April, Austria declared war, and by May, Giuseppina and Verdi at Sant'Agata could hear the gunfire of the French and Piedmontese soldiers fighting the Austrians only a few miles away. In June, Verdi started a relief fund for the wounded and their families. On September 15, Verdi and other delegates from Parma saw the king in Turin. Two days later, thanks to the friendly assistance of Sir James Hudson, the British Ambassador, Verdi met one of his idols, Count Camillo Cavour, whose fervor for Vittorio Emmanuele had helped convert Verdi the ardent republican to Verdi, loyal subject of the king.

89

*When the Duchy of Parma voted to unite with Piedmont, Verdi,
a leader in Italy's struggle to throw off the yoke of foreign
rule, was chosen to deliver the news to Victor Emanuel.
At that time he first met Cavour. Shown at left is the Piazza
del Duomo in Milan in 1859, lighted for the arrival of the king*

In 1861, when Italy finally achieved a partial, restless unification, Cavour overcame Verdi's resistance to the idea of standing for election from Busseto to the first Italian parliament. For a while Verdi had used that standard argument many artists have protested for centuries: "I am an artist, I have no knowledge of politics." Eventually he gave in, saying as he did so, "Blessed be the day when I can undeputize myself!" To no one's surprise, he was elected. In February he and Giuseppina went to Turin for the formal opening of the parliament, where Victor Emmanuel was declared king of Italy.

Once in, Verdi worked conscientiously at his new duties. In any voting he invariably followed Cavour's lead. Suddenly, in June, exhausted by his intensive political struggles, Cavour died. Giuseppina said that at the news Verdi cried "as he had at the death of his mother." With the death of the statesman whose insistence had been the real reason Verdi entered

Battles of the Risorgimento, such as Porta Tosa in Milan (right),
when barricades filled the streets, stirred Verdi to celebrate
war in many operas. He went to Russia in 1862 for the premiere
of La Forza del Destino *(above left), two years after Garibaldi*
(above right) and "the Thousand" had liberated Sicily and Naples

the political arena, the composer, already involved with plans for his next opera, removed himself from politics.

It was not merely to return to his farming and livestock that Verdi left the parliament at Turin. While he was still there he agreed to write an opera for the Imperial Theater in St. Petersburg. Choosing a Spanish play called *Don Alvaro, or, The Force of Destiny,* Verdi turned for what proved to be the last time to Piave for the libretto. Almost as soon as Piave started on his new assignment, it became clear that in the eighteen years of their collaboration the author had learned little of Verdi's preferences, and that Verdi had not modified his approach to Piave in the slightest.

"All the verses of the *terzetto* are quite bad," he wrote when the poet's first draft reached him. "One can't say that," he noted after one line. Of another line: "From there to the end everything must be done again."

Finally, " 'Maledetta'—and what does that mean?—must be changed to 'Ti maledico!' " And at last, after eight previous operas, "For God's sake, my dear Piave, let's think about this carefully. We can't go on like this: it's absolutely impossible with this drama."

But the bullying finally produced, as it always had, a finished text, and in November Verdi and Peppina, who had made elaborate advance preparations for their stay in St. Petersburg, took off on their longest trip.

But *Forza* was not given that season. Giuseppina explained the situation to Arrivabene in a letter from the Russian city dated February 1: "Alas! The voices of the singers are as frail as . . . (I leave you to finish this phrase), and the voice of Signora LaGrua is, to her and Verdi's misfortune, a desolating example of this fragility." So back to Sant'Agata they went, via London and Paris. They had hardly arrived when Verdi had to bury their beloved dog. He wrote Arrivabene, "Our Lulù, our poor little Lulù is dead! Poor little animal! My sadness is great, but Peppina is absolutely desolate!" The headstone Verdi put over Lulù's grave read, "To the memory of one of my most faithful friends."

The Imperial Theater in St. Petersburg, having paid Verdi 60,000 francs for the Russian rights to *Forza,* added a handsome bonus in November 1862, "an indemnity for having come twice to Russia," Giuseppina called it, and said it was "highly satisfactory." So was the opera as far as everyone was concerned. Peppina said the Czar and Czarina "smothered Verdi in compliments." A few days later the Czar sent Verdi the Order of St. Stanislas. The critic of the *Journal of St. Petersburg* wrote the day after the premiere about the "brilliant success of this beautiful work . . . magnificent score . . . the most complete, both in terms of its inspiration and the rich abundance of its melodic invention." Giuseppina noted that there were eight performances while she and Verdi were still in the city, all of them packed.

By now over a dozen Verdi operas had been heard in leading opera

La Forza del Destino at the Metropolitan Opera: Eugene Berman décor for the Convent Scene, 1952 (top); 1918 company premiere with José Mardones as Padre Guardiano, Enrico Caruso as Don Alvaro and Rosa Ponselle as Leonora (bottom left); Richard Tucker as Alvaro (center) and Zinka Milanov as Leonora (far right), stars of 1950s and 60s

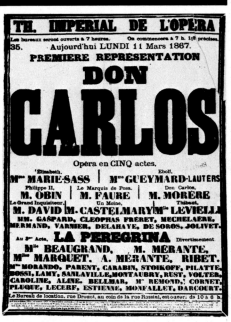

houses of Europe and America, where they were played not only in New York but in Boston, Philadelphia, Chicago, New Orleans and other cities. It seemed unlikely that any new opera by Verdi would be less than an instant success. Yet in March 1867, the day after the premiere of *Don Carlos,* which he had written for the Opéra to coincide with the exposition, Verdi wrote to Count Arrivabene, "Last night *Don Carlos.* It was not a success. I don't know what the future may hold, but I shouldn't be surprised if things were to change." Not a success? Other unsuccessful operas should be so lucky. In its first season in Paris *Don Carlos* (to use its French spelling) ran up a total of forty-three performances!

Actually, Verdi thought the initial cool response to the new opera was not so much a matter of the rumor that the Empress Eugénie did not like it (pity!) as that the performance did not come up to the standards he expected. Not long after, he wrote his French publisher and friend, Escudier. "It seems that *Don Carlos* has had a very great success in Bologna," he began. "Everybody says the performance is marvelous, and that there are some most powerful effects. I can't help reflecting: here it's not a month since rehearsals began, and the great effects are obtained; at the Opéra," recalling his problems at the time of the rehearsals for *Les Vêpres,* "they rehearse for eight months and the result in the end is an anemic and cold performance. See how right I am," he concludes, "to say that one single hand, if secure and powerful, can work miracles. You have seen it with Costa in London; you see it in greater measure with Mariani in Bologna."

After *Don Carlos* Verdi did not write another opera for four years. When he did, he was not present for its premiere. That took place in Cairo. The opera was *Aida.*

*   *   *

In January 1867, while Verdi was in Paris rehearsing for the opening of *Don Carlos,* his father, Carlo, died in Busseto. Giuseppina wrote to their friends telling them the news: "Verdi's father, an octogenarian and

Don Carlos, *staged in Paris in 1867, closed Verdi's middle period, hinting at dark splendors he would achieve in future works. Shown here are Feodor Chaliapin as King Philip (top), Giovanni Martinelli as Carlo (far left) and Raina Kabaivanska as Elisabetta with Grace Bumbry as Princess Eboli at the Metropolitan Opera*

ill for four years, ceased to suffer and rendered his soul to God in the night of the 14th of this month! . . . Verdi is extremely grieved."

Six months later, a much sadder loss was that in July of the man who had made everything possible for Verdi: Antonio Barezzi died at the age of seventy-nine. Verdi, whom he had loved as a son and admired for the genius he had always recognized, was at his side. This time Peppina wrote in her diary, "Farewell, beloved old man; our sorrow, our benedictions, our affection will follow you beyond the tomb. The memory of your goodness, and of all you did for Verdi, will be forgotten only when we in our turn close our eyes. Verdi presses your hands, and I press you to my heart. Farewell. Farewell."

The following summer Verdi met Alessandro Manzoni, the patriot and poet whose leadership in the Risorgimento had made him a Verdi idol. For the meeting the composer went to Milan, where he had not been in twenty years.

"Verdi was at Milan," Giuseppina wrote to the Countess Maffei, "after so many years' absence and such great desire on the part of his friends to see him again! He returned to that box at La Scala, witness of his first successes, of his struggles, of his first artistic experiences—those that are the frontispiece of the book of life for a man of genius!"

The long-standing ban on Verdi premieres at La Scala had never been lifted. But in February 1869 the composer supervised the first performance of the revised version of *Forza*. The Leonora was the Czech soprano Teresa Stolz, who from that moment on became increasingly important in the operas and the personal life of Verdi.

Meanwhile, Du Locle, the librettit of *Don Carlos,* had been besieging Verdi with one suggestion after another for an opera for Paris until Verdi finally wrote him. Speaking of the "fatal atmosphere" of the Opéra, he concluded, "I'm no composer for Paris. I don't know whether or not I lack the talent, but certainly my ideas about art are very different from

Aida, though written for the opening of the Suez Canal, was not given in Cairo until Christmas Eve 1871. Here are famous interpreters of the heroine: Teresa Stolz, La Scala 1872; Emma Eames, turn-of-the-century Metropolitan Opera; Leontyne Price of Scala and Met, 1960s and 70s; Emmy Destinn, Met 1908; Elisabeth Rethberg, Met 1920s and 30s

AIDA

OPERA IN QUATTRO ATTI

VERSI DI A. GHISLANZONI

MUSICA DI

G. VERDI

CANTO E PIANOFORTE — PIANOFORTE SOLO

IN QUARTO (s) Lire 50.   IN QUARTO (s) Lire 30.
IN OTTAVO »   30.   IN OTTAVO »   15.

PIANOFORTE A QUATTRO MANI (s) Lire 100.—

G. RICORDI E C.

MILANO - ROMA - NAPOLI - PALERMO - LONDRA
LIPSIA - BUENOS AIRES - SAN PAULO (Brasile)
PARIS - SOC. ANON. DES ÉDITIONS RICORDI
NEW YORK - G. RICORDI & C., INC.

those of your country. I believe in inspiration; you believe in construction."

That did not stop Du Locle. One day he sent Verdi a fairly detailed synopsis of an opera set in the Egypt of the pharaohs. Verdi was interested (actually he was hooked, though he did not quite realize it). The sketch was by a French Egyptologist named Auguste Mariette. What's more, the Khedive of Egypt had agreed to Mariette's idea of commissioning an opera based on the sketch to celebrate the coming opening of the Suez Canal. Would Signor Verdi be interested? He would, especially in view of the high fees that were in sight.

By the time all the arrangements had been made, however, the Suez Canal was open. So was the Cairo Opera House, for the opening of which also it had been suggested that Signor Verdi should write an opera. The

*In early years of this century, Louise Homer as Amneris (above left)
and Enrico Caruso as Radames (above right) were indispensable to Aida
at the Metropolitan Opera. During the 1962-63 season, La Scala, Milan,
introduced a spectacular new production evoking stagings from Verdi's
era designed by Lila de Nobili and directed by Franco Zeffirelli (right)*

opera house opened on November 1, 1869, not with a new opera but with *Rigoletto*. What with one delay and another, one of which was the Franco-Prussian War, it was not until Christmas Eve 1871 that the world first heard what was to become the most popular opera of all time.

Verdi was not present the night they first played *Aida*. He did not want to make the trip, and he was already at work preparing for the premiere of *Aida* at La Scala, to take place in February. Verdi had no doubts about the worth of his new opera. "I don't want to play modest with you," he wrote Arrivabene the day after the Scala premiere. "This is by no means the worst thing I've written, and time will give it the place it deserves. In short, it's a success and will pack the theater. If I'm wrong I'll write to you. Meanwhile, farewell in haste."

For La Scala and Stolz he conceived the great scene that begins "O

The world's most popular opera, Aida *holds a record of 603 performances at the Metropolitan Opera through the 1976-77 season. The company's new production in 1976, staged by John Dexter and designed by David Reppa and Peter J. Hall, is shown at left: Marilyn Horne as Amneris (top), the Act II finale (bottom), with Cornell MacNeil (Amonasro), Leontyne Price (Aida), James Morris (King), Bonaldo Giaiotti (Ramfis), Horne (Amneris) and James McCracken (Radames). Above is the Soviet mezzo-soprano Elena Obraztsova as Amneris in the judgment scene*

patria mia." From details included in his letter to Arrivabene, Verdi was thoroughly satisfied with the way La Scala met the challenge of its first Verdi premiere in a quarter of a century. "Performance of ensemble and soloists excellent," he said. "Production also . . . orchestra and chorus fine."

He was right about *Aida* packing the theater, too. For over a century it has been packing opera theaters; no other opera has been given so often at the Metropolitan, where *Aida* has by now passed the 600 mark. Surely, after so unqualified a success, Verdi would write another opera in the shortest possible time. But no. Although more and better were still to come, fifteen years would pass before another Verdi opera was heard.

The Messa da Requiem *was heard at La Scala after the premiere, with soloists Giuseppe Capponi, Ormondo Maini, Maria Waldmann and Teresa Stolz, Verdi conducting (below). In 1967 Herbert von Karajan led the work there with Leontyne Price, Shirley Verrett, Luciano Pavarotti and Nicolai Ghiaurov as the soloists (right)*

VIII

THE GREAT COLLABORATION: VERDI, BOITO,

THOSE who enjoy playing at anagrams love the name of the man who was librettist for Ponchielli's *Gioconda* and Verdi's last two operas, *Otello* and *Falstaff*. Tobia Gorrio wrote the former, Arrigo Boito the last two.

In 1862, when Boito at the age of twenty had written the verses Verdi needed for his *Hymn of the Nations,* it would have required genuine clairvoyance for anyone to foresee the combination Boito and Verdi as one of the great collaborations in opera history. And after an unfortunate night in November 1863, anyone rash enough to ask about the possibility of mutual efforts between the two men would have been run out of the Verdi household.

Boito was a close friend of Franco Faccio, a composer of slender

The bedroom of Verdi's home in Sant'Agata became filled with career mementos, including a petit-point chair of Aida *design. On one wall is the famous bust of the composer by the sculptor Vincenzo Gemito (top left). Nearby, in the bedroom of Giuseppina, is a painting of her beloved dog, Lulù (top right)*

talents but a man who would become what Harold Rosenthal calls "the first great modern Italian opera conductor." It was he who would conduct the Scala premiere of *Aida,* which so satisfied Verdi. In 1863, however, Faccio's opera *I Profughi Fiamminghi* had its premiere at La Scala. At the post-curtain party thrown for Faccio by his friends, Boito got up and read an ode in which he announced that the state of music in Italy was a mess. "Perhaps the man is already born who will restore art, in its purity, on the altar now defiled like the wall of a brothel," Boito enthusiastically declaimed. These rousing sentiments might have sounded great to the partygoers, particularly after the first few bottles of the local produce had been opened and downed. To Verdi, however, reading them in cold print a few days later, they reeked of juvenile ignorance. To the man with twenty-two operas behind him they were a personal insult.

For years he kept bringing them up and complaining about them to his friends and colleagues. "If I too, among the others, have soiled the altar, as Boito says," he would growl, "let him clean it and I shall be the first to come and light a candle."

An opera by Verdi to a libretto by Boito? Never!

However—if Verdi could be stubborn, Giulio Ricordi could be persistent and Giuseppina ingenious. And these two highly influential people

were subtly working to heal the wound. It helped a bit that Verdi was growing to admire Faccio's conducting and to like him personally. Faccio, after all, might have been the occasion for the ode, but he was not its author. Years passed, nevertheless, before Verdi entirely abandoned his enmity toward Boito. In the end it was neither Ricordi nor Giuseppina, for all the skill with which they prepared Verdi for a reconciliation, to whom the final credit must go. It belongs to Shakespeare.

It was Ricordi who first suggested the idea of a Boito libretto based on a play by Shakespeare. No matter what his opinion of Boito as a writer of youthful odes, Verdi had never had any doubts about his skill as a librettist. The composer declined to discuss the matter with the two interested parties. "I wish absolutely to avoid committing myself," he wrote the publisher, adding that any visit from Ricordi and Boito would "commit me too much."

When Boito himself finally brought the composer a sketch for an opera on the subject of *Otello,* Verdi told him, "Write the libretto. It will come in handy for yourself, for me or for someone else." Gradually Verdi let himself be drawn more and more into the scheme, protesting all the way. He told Ricordi he would be glad to read over "a finished poem and give my opinion calmly, without committing either party." On

Arrigo Boito (far left), composer of Mefistofele, *prepared Verdi's last librettos, brilliant adaptations from Shakespeare,* Otello *and* Falstaff. *Shown at left is the first* Otello, *Francesco Tamagno, in his death scene*

November 18, 1879, Verdi received a completed libretto. He read it. He bought it. And for nearly five years he let it rest beside his bed before he began to compose music for it!

He did not, however, wait five years before getting to work with Boito. Falling in with Ricordi's firm belief that only certain revisions were needed to make a success of *Boccanegra,* which had languished in relative obscurity since its 1857 premiere, Verdi agreed that Boito might be able to make something out of the infirmities of Piave's libretto. Boito, with remarkable magnanimity, was willing to try. And Verdi, finding himself at last working with a creative genius, found ways of writing to Boito rather different from those he had used in his correspondence with Piave, Solera and Cammarano. "Immersed in more important work and thinking of *Otello,*" he wrote while they were involved with the repairs to *Boccanegra,* "you are aiming here at an unobtainable perfection. I do not aim so high and so am more optimistic than you, and by no means in despair. I admit the table is shaky, but if we adjust the legs a little I think it will stand up."

And stand up it did, quite gloriously, in March 1881, when it was heard in its new guise at La Scala. With the wholly new council chamber scene, Boito had given the composer a grand opportunity, and the post-*Aida* Verdi had used it to create one of his most telling episodes.

In February 1883, Verdi was shaken to hear of the death in Venice of Richard Wagner, the other great operatic giant of the century, who was born the same year as he. Despite some reservations he had always held about Wagner's working methods, he wrote Ricordi, saying, "Sad, sad, sad. Wagner is dead! When I read the news yesterday, I may truly say I was completely crushed. Let us not discuss it. It is a great personality that has disappeared. A name which leaves a mighty imprint upon the history of art."

In March 1884, when Verdi was seventy, he began to write the music for *Otello.* By October 1885 he had finished it except for the scoring and

In 1972 the Metropolitan Opera unveiled a striking new production of Otello *by designer-director Franco Zeffirelli. Shown here are the moonlit harbor of Act I with Teresa Zylis-Gara (Desdemona) and Jon Vickers (Otello) and the Act III finale with Jean Kraft (Emilia), Zylis-Gara, Vickers and Louis Quilico (Iago)*

some revisions. In December 1886 he sent Ricordi's the final score pages of what many consider the greatest of all Verdi operas. Some go beyond the purely musical achievement and say that the Boito-Verdi *Otello* is a greater work than the Shakespeare *Othello*.

Even Verdi had never seen anything like the night *Otello* had its premiere at La Scala, February 5, 1887. He and Boito enjoyed ovations that outdid those of any previous Verdi triumph. Called out twenty times, Verdi saw the entire audience on its feet, waving hats and handkerchiefs. Many were weeping with excitement. Verdi was presented with a silver album that held autographs and cards from every citizen of Milan!

When he left the theater, his carriage was pulled by eager admirers. He was toasted and serenaded until five in the morning. He even complained he could not sleep for the shouts of "Viva Verdi!"

What a magnificent ending to a grand career in the world of opera. Only it was not the end. For years no one dared think that another opera would follow *Otello*—no one, that is, except the insatiable Ricordi, the faithful Boito, the devoted Giuseppina and surely the great old man also. Not that he gave any sign there might ever be another Verdi premiere. He spent his time and energy helping to build a hospital near Sant'Agata; he helped bring in a system of irrigation; he reduced his tenants' rents.

But—always that nagging thought—what if? What if Boito could produce another miracle, another ideal libretto? And Boito did. By midsummer, two and a half years after the great night when *Otello* opened, Verdi was reading with vast relish a libretto called *Falstaff*. Another play of Shakespeare! And as if to wash away all the hurt that had followed his first and last try at comedy, this was a brilliant, witty book.

Verdi was now seventy-six. But his exuberance was youthful when he wrote to Boito, "What a joy to be able to say to the public, HERE WE ARE AGAIN!! COME AND SEE US!!" To Ricordi, however, he hauled out the old warnings: "I am writing *Falstaff* to pass the time, nothing else." And later, "I believe it ought to be performed at Sant'Agata and not at La Scala." But by September 1892 he had finished it.

Even then, Verdi hedged his new creation around with stiff prohibitions, suggesting that if at the last moment of final rehearsal he was not satisfied, he would withdraw the work. Nothing like this happened. On February 9, 1893, six years after the premiere of *Otello* and eight months before Verdi's eightieth birthday, *Falstaff* brought Verdi once more the unstinting bravos of the world of music and the general public. "Admirers, bores, friends, enemies, genuine and non-genuine musicians," Giuseppina wrote to her sister, "critics good and bad are swarming in

Shown far left in the garden at Sant'Agata are Maria Filomena Carrera, Barberina Strepponi, the aging Verdi, Mrs. Giulio Ricordi (all seated), Teresa Stolz, lawyer Campanari, Ricordi, painter Meclovicz (all standing). At left is the courtyard of what Verdi called "My finest work," the Casa di Riposo, a home for aged musicians he founded in Milan

Falstaff *was first given at La Scala in 1893, with Victor Maurel as Sir John (below). At left, Tito Gobbi as Falstaff and Renata Tebaldi as Alice at the Metropolitan Opera. Below, the finale with Tebaldi (Alice), Regina Resnik (Quickly), Luigi Alva (Fenton), Andrea Velis (Bardolph), Geraint Evans (Falstaff), Richard Best (Pistol), Jeannette Pilou (Nannetta), Joann Grillo (Meg) and Paul Franke (Caius)*

from all over the world. The way people are clamoring for seats, the opera house would have to be as big as a public square."

They all loved it, this thing full of sparkling light, of champagne-like explosions and instantaneous shifts in mood, this story of teenage love by a man five times as old as his young lovers. At its center stands Sir John, whom Verdi's music gives a new humanity even while it underscores his heavy drinking, his unabashed wenching, his monstrous ego.

Of all the miracles Verdi wrought, this one in his eightieth year is the most astonishing. But as he liked to point out, the thread that runs through his operas (and his Requiem) can be traced from *Nabucco* and *Ernani* straight through to *Otello* and *Falstaff*. The seeds that were planted so early grew into magnificent trees.

Not all those trees were operatic. In May 1872, fifteen months after the Scala premiere of *Aida,* another of Verdi's idols died. Alessandro Manzoni had been both one of Italy's greatest writers and a fervent fighter for the Risorgimento. It had been to meet Manzoni that Verdi returned to Milan after avoiding the city for over twenty years.

"Now all is over," Verdi wrote when he heard of Manzoni's death. "With him ends the most pure, the most holy, the greatest of all our glories." Within two weeks of the writer's death, Verdi wrote the mayor of Milan to say he would compose a Requiem Mass for Manzoni. He suggested that the first performance be given on the first anniversary of Manzoni's death. By April 1874 Verdi had finished the score. On May 22, in the Church of San Marco, he conducted its first performance. Within a year Verdi would conduct the Requiem fifteen times in Paris, four in Vienna and three in London. Coming shortly after *Aida* and fourteen years before *Otello*, the Requiem has the strengths of past Verdi triumphs and clear foreshadowings of the great things yet to come.

It was in March 1873 that Verdi wrote his only piece of chamber

Twenty-six operas and the Messa da Requiem *are Verdi's major legacy to music-lovers. The dog-eared scores shown here are the composer's own, standing in his workroom at Sant'Agata. The music in these volumes reflects Verdi's own arrow-straight integrity as well as the passionate spirit of his native land*

music, a string quartet of great charm, a score that could have come from no other hand. It is, incidentally, sometimes heard played by full string orchestra, an idea Verdi is said to have liked.

The last music ever to come from Verdi's pen was a setting of the Stabat Mater, one of a set of *Four Sacred Pieces* published in 1898. They were not, however, written at one time. The first two, an "Ave Maria" and "Laudi alla Vergine," were composed between *Otello* and *Falstaff*. In 1895, while he was busy with plans for the building of a rest home for musicians in Milan, Verdi finished a setting of the Te Deum Laudamus and the Stabat Mater. With these his music-making ended forever. Two years later, in November 1897, his lifetime companion Giuseppina died. "Now farewell, my Verdi," her will concluded. "As we were united in life, may God join our spirits together again in heaven."

Three years and two months later, at the age of eighty-seven, Verdi died in his suite at the Grand Hotel in Milan, where he had spent Christmas with Boito, Stolz and Giulio Ricordi. The great old man had asked that a copy of his Te Deum be buried with him. He had also asked for a funeral with no music, no singing. But the love of the people of Milan for Verdi was too great to say farewell to him in silence. As his coffin was being laid next to Giuseppina's in the ground of the municipal cemetery, someone in the crowd that thronged the place began to sing. Softly the words and music rose in the winter air as, gradually, everyone joined in: "Và, pensiero, sull'ali dorate. . . ."

THE VERDI REPERTORY

STORIES OF THE OPERAS

Compiled by Stephen Wadsworth

OBERTO, CONTE DI SAN BONIFACIO

ACT I.   The action takes place in Bassano in 1228. In her brother's castle, Cuniza's impending marriage is celebrated by a group of friends, who welcome her affianced, Riccardo, Count of Salinguerra, from the wars. Leonora, daughter of the banished Oberto, Count of San Bonifacio, enters later, ruminating on her seduction and betrayal by this same Riccardo and her father's subsequent disowning of her. When she is gone, Oberto himself appears, having risked death to return to his homeland. He hears a voice muttering that the wedding will take place that night and turns to find his daughter. At first he shuns Leonora, who disgraced his name, but readmits her to his affections when she swears by her mother in heaven that she desires to avenge her belittlement by Riccardo.

Although Cuniza is feted imperially by her cheerful ladies-in-waiting, she feels a foreboding of unhappiness. She shares this with Riccardo, who bids her forget and paints a bright picture of their future. Leonora, heart pounding, requests an audience with Cuniza, relating her entire tale of woe to the astonished girl, who undertakes to confront her fiancé on the spot. She sees Oberto out and calls in her guests, pointing an accusatory finger at Riccardo. When he reverses the charge, accusing Leonora of falseness, Leonora vigorously protests and wins the favor of the on-lookers. The most convincing testimony, however, is that of Oberto, who now seconds his daughter and challenges the mortified Riccardo.

ACT II. Cuniza smothers her personal disappointment in kindness to Leonora, who she feels must reclaim Riccardo. She even refuses to see him, averring that his duty is to his earlier love. She admits Leonora, whom she apprises of her friendly intentions. But Cuniza will only help Leonora if she can be sure that the girl is truly blameless; Leonora swears that she is, and the women embrace affectionately. [This duet appears at the end of the autograph score.]

Oberto impatiently awaits Riccardo's response to his challenge. He learns that Cuniza has interceded with her brother to terminate his exile, but before he leaves to thank her, Oberto inveighs against Riccardo, saying that vengeance is still uppermost in his mind. Riccardo arrives and wishes not to combat the older man; Oberto's accusation of cowardice does the trick, but Riccardo sheathes his sword when Cuniza and Leonora both descend from the castle to stop them. Riccardo agrees to marry Leonora, as Cuniza insists, but Oberto isn't yet willing to forget the matter of his honor and he draws off Riccardo after the ladies return to the castle. A group of knights conversing in the courtyard are alarmed by a cry from the direction of the forest. Rushing off to investigate, they do not see Riccardo, who now enters. The sword in his hand has killed Oberto, which is no comfort to the broken man. He departs, downcast and sad. Cuniza appears to find that her forebodings were warranted; when Leonora hears the news, it is almost too much for her. A letter from Riccardo, who has left Italy, never to return, leaves all his possessions to her in recognition of her claim to him. Cuniza and her maids try to calm Leonora.

UN GIORNO DI REGNO (IL FINTO STANISLAO)

ACT I.   It is 1733. In Baron Kelbar's castle near Brest, the staff joyfully anticipates a double wedding: the Baron's daughter Giulietta will marry Gasparo Antonio della Rocca, the Treasurer of the States of Brittany (for his money), and the Baron's niece, the Marchesa of Poggio, will marry Count Ivrea, the Commandant of Brest. Both girls are in love with other men—Giulietta with the Treasurer's nephew Edoardo and the Marchesa with the Cavalier Belfiore. Since Belfiore, actually her fiancé, has apparently left her, the Marchesa will marry Count Ivrea out of spite. Stanislao, King of Poland, is announced and welcomed. This is Belfiore, posing as Stanislao so that the real king can journey discreetly to Warsaw. When he is told that the Marchesa is soon to be wed, Belfiore excuses the company and writes to Warsaw asking to be released from his mission to save his love affair. The unhappy Edoardo enters, begging to be of use to the King now that he cannot marry his beloved. With some pomp, Belfiore engages him as an attaché and they leave. The Marchesa tiptoes in and has a good look at the King, quite certain that it is Belfiore. She decides to go through with her marriage and see if it flushes Belfiore out of his pose.

In a garden, Giulietta yields to depression thinking about her ancient fiancé (the Treasurer) and yearning for Edoardo. The Baron approaches with the Treasurer and introduces his daughter to the King, the latter attended by Edoardo. Belfiore prevails upon the Baron and the Treasurer for military advice, seating them with their backs to Edoardo, who is free to converse with his girlfriend. When the Marchesa advances, she too is introduced to the King, whose uncanny resemblance to her cavalier startles her anew. The Baron and the Treasurer draw out Belfiore, titillated by the notion of promotion, and leave with him. The lovers appeal to the Marchesa for help, but she is too agitated to be much help to anyone. Soon, however, she rallies, because being in love herself, she understands their feelings.

Back in the castle, Belfiore suggests the Treasurer marry a Polish princess instead of Giulietta; of course the venal Treasurer agrees, but in putting down the Baron's daughter, he must put up with the Baron's wrath. They argue loudly, soon joined by the lovers, who now want to be wed (an idea advanced by the Marchesa). All of this creates an immense amount of noise, and Belfiore reenters looking fierce. The company is embarrassed. The "King" agrees to judge the situation.

ACT II. In a gallery, Edoardo cheers up the servants with his optimistic view of the outcome. Belfiore brings in the Treasurer and requires that he give up a large sum and one of his estates to Edoardo in order that the youth have a fine chance of winning Giulietta's hand. The Treasurer is hardly in a position to refuse; he again arouses the animosity of the Baron and they shout at each other, full of baroque threats.

In an interview with the King, the Marchesa is still not able to discern for sure whether he is her man, but she does put a fire under Belfiore when she makes clear her intention to marry Count Ivrea. As that gentleman arrives, the Marchesa intimates to Belfiore that she will reconsider her decision should her real boyfriend come out of the woodwork.

Giulietta and Edoardo enter the empty hall. Their joy at being officially reunited is marred by Edoardo's job with the Polish luminary which requires him to travel. In come the Baron, Count Ivrea and the Marchesa and, eventually, Belfiore, who goes about delaying the weddings by pretending to call Count Ivrea off on a secret mission. The ensuing din cools off when a messenger from the court of Poland arrives with a letter for

Belfiore. The real King of Poland has arrived in Warsaw and been recognized by his Parliament; Belfiore has been made a Marshal for his services. While everybody promises to forget everything, Belfiore throws his arms around the Marchesa.

NABUCCO

ACT I. JERUSALEM.   Six hundred years before the birth of Christ, a group of terrified Hebrews at the Temple of Solomon pray for deliverance from Nabucco, mighty King of Assyria, who is attacking their city. The High Priest Zaccaria leads in Nabucco's daughter Fenena, who has been captured and is held as hostage; Zaccaria assures the Hebrews that Nabucco will halt the attack when he learns that his daughter is in their hands. Ismaele, nephew of the King of Jerusalem, enters with his legions to announce that Nabucco is at the gates, whereupon Zaccaria places Fenena in the youth's custody and rushes off with the others to join the battle. Left alone, the two young people recall how Fenena had saved Ismaele from the wrath of her wicked sister Abigaille when he himself was a prisoner of the Assyrians. As he promises to set Fenena free, Abigaille, followed by a band of her soldiers, enters brandishing her sword. Though she vows to save his people if he will return her love, Ismaele scorns her. The Hebrews crowd into the temple pursued by the victorious Nabucco and his warriors. When Zaccaria threatens to stab Fenena in retaliation, Ismaele seizes the dagger; the young man laments his treachery amid the curses of the Israelites. Nabucco swears he will show no mercy to the Hebrews.

ACT II. THE PAGAN.   In a room of Nabucco's palace in Babylon, Abigaille reads a secret scroll that reveals her true identity—she is not Nabucco's daughter, but a slave. In fear and rage, she plots vengeance on the king, now departed for further conquests, and on Fenena, who has been appointed regent in his absence. Confronted by the High Priest of Baal, Abigaille learns that Fenena has liberated the Hebrews and that Nabucco has fallen in battle. Joyfully she vows to seize the throne.

Later that night, Zaccaria and a Levite bearing the Tablets of Moses steal into the palace, declaring that Jehovah has commanded him to convert Fenena to Judaism, and the priest enters her room. More Levites appear, followed by Ismaele, who begs their forgiveness but is still reviled. He asks for death. Fenena emerges with Anna and Zaccaria, who announce that she has been converted. Suddenly Abdallo, Nabucco's servant, hurries in to warn Fenena that the Assyrian king is reported slain and that his people have proclaimed Abigaille their queen. Before Fenena can flee, Abigaille and her cohorts enter, demanding that she surrender the crown. To their astonishment, Nabucco bursts in and seizes the crown for himself, declaring that he is not only their king but their god as well. At these words a bolt of lightning strikes Nabucco mad. As the Hebrews cry out that heaven has punished the blasphemer, Abigaille takes up the crown.

ACT III. THE PROPHECY AND THE BROKEN IDOL. On the bank of the Euphrates, the enchained Hebrews dream of their homeland. When Zaccaria prophesies the fall of Babylon, they all hope for freedom.

On Nabucco's throne, Abigaille accepts the homage of Babylonians. The High Priest of Baal approaches her and demands death for the Jews and the converted Fenena; suddenly Nabucco enters the hall. Although the faithful Abdallo tries to lead him away, he insists on addressing Abigaille. Dismissing the court, she persuades Nabucco to seal a death warrant for the Hebrews. Unaware that in so doing he seals Fenena's doom, the deranged monarch agrees. At once Abigaille gives the guards the execution decree. The horrified Nabucco, pleading for his daughter's life, threatens to reveal Abigaille's slave birth, at which she whips forth the secret scroll and destroys it before his eyes. A fanfare heralds the execution of the Hebrews; Nabucco orders the guards to arrest Abigaille, but she laughs that their charge is Nabucco himself. Still begging for mercy for Fenena, he is led to his cell. Abigaille swears that, though a slave, she will not bring dishonor on the crown of Assyria.

Brooding on his past glory, Nabucco mistakes shouts in the street outside his cell for a battle call. When he rushes to his barred window he sees Fenena being dragged to execution. In despair the king falls on his knees, imploring the aid of Jehovah, the god he once despised. As if in answer to this prayer, Abdallo breaks in with soldiers and Nabucco hurries them off to rescue daughter and throne.

At the altar of Baal the Hebrews are brought for execution. No sooner has Fenena told Zaccaria that her new faith strengthens her to face death than Nabucco's legions swarm in. The king orders the destruction of the idol of Baal, but supernatural powers intervene and shatter it before his soldiers can act. Abigaille, who has taken poison, stumbles dying from the throne, imploring forgiveness for her crimes. Jehovah has restored sanity to Nabucco, who orders the Israelites to return to Jerusalem and rebuild their temple. All kneel before the power of the Hebrew god.

I LOMBARDI ALLA PRIMA CROCIATA

ACT I. THE REVENGE. 1099. In the square before the Church of Sant' Ambrogio in Milan, citizens tell the story of Lord Folco's sons, once rival suitors for the hand of Viclinda. Pagano lost the girl to Arvino and a subsequent murder attempt on his brother earned him exile. Now Pagano has returned and a reconciliation is enacted, though the crowd and Arvino's family correctly suspect Pagano of further wrongdoing. Alone, Pagano proves his villainy, deriding a distant nuns' prayer and plotting with his henchman Pirro to murder Arvino and abduct Viclinda.

Old Folco is spending the night in Arvino's apartments because his son is uneasy for his safety. Viclinda kneels to pray with her daughter, Giselda. Soon Pagano and his band infiltrate, but with intent to kill Arvino, Pagano dispatches his father in Arvino's bed. The guards prevent the wretched Pagano from committing suicide and all denounce him.

ACT II. THE MAN OF THE CAVE.   In his Antioch palace, the tyrant Acciano vows to repel the invading crusaders. When the room is empty, his wife Sofia approaches with her son, Oronte, who has fallen in love with Giselda, imprisoned in Acciano's harem. Sofia, secretly a Christian convert, is pleased when Oronte says he wants to embrace the faith of his beloved.

In the surrounding desert, a Hermit devotes his life to God's will to expunge past crimes, hoping for the chance to prove his mettle in the Crusade. A Moslem appears seeking penance from the famous holy man for his sins—his part in a parricide, his flight from Lombardy and the renunciation of his faith. The Hermit encourages his supplicator, actually Pirro, to open Antioch's gate to the crusaders, then hides him in his cave as Lombard troops draw near. The Hermit emerges in armor, visor down, to meet the intruders. Their leader, Arvino, seeks advice from the great holy man; his daughter has been taken prisoner and all rescue attempts have failed. The Hermit undertakes to lead the Lombards into Antioch, where father will find daughter and Christians will enjoy victory.

In the harem, Giselda's desperate prayer is interrupted by battling Turks and crusaders. Sofia points to the crusaders who slew her husband and her son—Arvino. Disgusted by the inhuman carnage around her, Giselda refuses to greet her father, determined that God could not condone a holocaust in His name. The Hermit prevents Arvino from striking the girl down, saying that grief has replaced her reason.

ACT III. THE CONVERSION.   As the echo of pilgrims and crusaders praising Jerusalem trail away, Giselda comes from her father's tent, full of anxiety. She is astonished when Oronte appears before her. Explaining that Arvino's swordblow only rendered him unconscious, he accepts Giselda's offer to follow him through thick and thin and they flee when a call to arms is heard from the camp.

Arvino, cursing his daughter's escape, is informed that Pagano has been seen in the encampment. Seeing this as an ill omen, Arvino rallies his men in a vengeful search for the offender.

In a grotto near the Jordan, Giselda succors the wounded Oronte. Disconsolate, she reproves God for his cruelty. The Hermit presents himself as if in answer to her rebuke: she must not accuse God. He then baptizes Oronte, who dies in the comfort of the true faith.

ACT IV. THE HOLY SEPULCHRE. In a cave near Jerusalem, Giselda has a dream in which the heavenly spirit of Oronte reveals the whereabouts of a spring to restore the thirsting crusaders. Giselda leads them to Siloam, where they strengthen themselves and prepare for victory.

The Hermit has been fatally wounded and lurches into Arvino's tent dying. Finally he shows his face to Arvino and Giselda: he is Pagano. His family forgives him and grants his wish to see the Holy City, which stands in the blazing sun, decked with the triumphant banners of the Crusade.

ERNANI

ACT I. THE BANDIT. In the mountains of Aragon, about 1519, outlaws gather about their leader, the proscribed nobleman Ernani, who tells them that his beloved Elvira must marry her elderly uncle, Don Ruy Gomez de Silva. Revealing that Silva has detained Elvira in a nearby castle, Ernani secures the help of his men in rescuing her.

That evening, as the lady Elvira impatiently awaits her lover, Ernani, in a courtyard of Silva's castle, she is visited by another suitor, Charles I of Spain (Carlo), who passionately declares his love. When the king tries to abduct her, Elvira snatches his dagger in self-defense. Ernani suddenly leaps from the battlements, and Carlo—who has confiscated the outlaw's possessions and killed his father—taunts him with insults. The two men are about to duel when Silva bursts in and is shocked to discover Elvira with strangers. Just then the royal standard-bearer's arrival reveals Carlo's identity to the astonished Silva, who pays him homage. The king announces that he will spend the night in the castle and dismisses Ernani as a mere retainer. Smarting under this insult, Ernani mutters hatred but is urged by Elvira to flee.

ACT II. THE GUEST.   In the magnificent courtyard of Silva's palace, festivities are in progress for his marriage to Elvira. Ernani appears, disguised as a pilgrim, and is extended the hospitality of the house by Silva himself. When Elvira enters in bridal dress, Ernani throws aside his cloak and offers his own head, on which a price has been set, as a wedding gift. Elvira, left alone for a moment with her lover, assures him she would have killed herself rather than marry Silva, who returns to find the couple embracing. Such is the old man's code of honor, however, that when the king approaches, Silva conceals Ernani in a chapel rather than betray his presence. Carlo furiously accuses Silva of harboring the outlaw, whereupon the old man offers his own head as forfeit. When Elvira rushes in to beg mercy of the king, he secretly renews his declaration of love and departs with her as hostage. Silva now demands satisfaction of Ernani, but the bandit reveals to the astonished grandee that the king also is a suitor for Elvira's hand. As a token of faith, Ernani gives his hunting horn to Silva, promising to kill himself whenever the old man sounds it. Temporarily united in Elvira's cause, the two men rush off to fight the king.

ACT III. CLEMENCY.   At Charlemagne's tomb in Aix-la-Chapelle, Carlo, awaiting the electors' choice for the next Holy Roman Emperor, meditates on the futility of wealth and power. He disappears into the tomb as conspirators gather to choose his assassin. Ernani is selected; refusing to yield his task to Silva, he again provokes the old man's wrath. As booming cannon announce that Carlo has been selected emperor, the king emerges from hiding and orders the assembled electorate to punish the conspirators, imprisoning commoners and beheading nobles. Ernani steps from the crowd to declare himself Don Juan of Aragon, whereupon Elvira once again beseeches mercy of Carlo. Addressing himself to the spirit of Charlemagne, the new emperor grants clemency to the conspirators and agrees to further the marriage of Ernani and Elvira. Silva broods on revenge.

ACT IV. THE MASKER.   At the palace of Don Juan of Aragon, as a masked ball celebrates the nobleman's approaching wedding, a mysterious stranger haunts the terrace. Ernani and Elvira, leaving the merrymakers for a moment, fall into each other's arms. Three times a distant horn sounds, interrupting their idyll. Ernani feigns illness and sends the terrified Elvira for a physician; then he confronts Silva, who has torn off his mask. Ernani pleads for a moment of happiness at the end of his life of misery, but the old man insists that the sinister compact be fulfilled. Offered a dagger, Ernani stabs himself and falls dying in Elvira's arms as Silva pronounces his vengeance squared.

I DUE FOSCARI

ACT I.   In a hall of the Doge's palace, citizens hail the Venice of 1457 and those who rule her as the Council of Ten assembles in their chamber. An officer leaves Jacopo Foscari behind bars to await sentence. Son of the octogenarian Doge Francesco Foscari, Jacopo has endured exile twice, once for dealing with foreign leaders, once when accused of arranging the assassination of a previous Council head, Ermalao Donato. His secret return to his beloved Venice has been uncovered and he is now under arrest. Secure though he is in his innocence, Jacopo fears the Ten can be swayed by Jacopo Loredano, enemy to his father the Doge. The officer returns to summon Jacopo Foscari before the Council of Ten.

Lucrezia, Jacopo's wife, rushes into a hall in the Foscari palace, intent on begging the old Doge to intervene. Her prayers are met only with her confidant's news that Jacopo's exile has been reestablished. Lucrezia is furious with the Council and calls down God's judgment on them.

Meanwhile, the Ten are dispersing into the loggia in the Doge's palace. Their comments reveal that Jacopo's treasonous reputation was further damaged by his appeal to the Duke of Milan for intercession in the matter of his regaining favor in Venice. The Ten believe their judgment has been fair.

After bemoaning his son's fate and his own powerlessness before the Ten, the old Doge welcomes Lucrezia to his apartments. She cannot fathom why Francesco condemned his own son knowing the vengeful tactics of the Ten. The old man is very moved by her torment, but explains Jacopo's entreaty to Milan is unavoidably a crime; he as Doge must uphold the law. The two weep together.

ACT II. In a cell in the state prison, Jacopo is visited by hallucinations, including the specter of another man wrongly condemned. Lucrezia descends to find him in a delirium. The sight of his wife overjoys him, though he must lament the exile which will send him again far from her and from his children. Francesco joins them, professing his love for his son and exhorting him to have faith in ultimate justice from heaven. Husband and wife heap invective on the cold, evil Loredano when he appears to send Jacopo to the ship. Leaning on Lucrezia, the old Doge follows the procession out.

Before the Council of Ten and the Doge, Jacopo reads the decree that banishes him. Lucrezia arrives with her children and throws herself on the mercy of the court. The Doge is crushed, but although the senator

Barbarigo begs Loredano to be sensible, Jacopo is separated from his family and removed in custody.

ACT III.   Crowds mill in the Piazza San Marco, anticipating the regatta with pride and celebration. When the people have followed the race off the scene, Jacopo is escorted from the Ducal palace. In his farewell to Lucrezia, he says that his only hope now is death and begs her to stifle back her tears and show herself a noblewoman. Loredano exults in their pain and parting.

The Doge's lamentations are interrupted by Barbarigo, who bursts in to say that another man has confessed on his deathbed to the slaying of Donato. His joy is killed when Lucrezia discloses that Jacopo died on departure: it is too late. Moreover, the Ten approach in ceremony to address Francesco, whom they relieve of his princely duties, maneuvered by Loredano. The old man is shocked when bells betoken a salute to his successor, already chosen, and he collapses in anguish, dead.

GIOVANNA D'ARCO

PROLOGUE.   Downcast courtiers, villagers and soldiers wait anxiously in the royal courtyard at Domrémy (c. 1429) for Carlo (Charles VII), the uncrowned Dauphin. He enters and utters his final command: the French must lay down their swords and cede power to the English king. A vision of a painted statue of the Virgin came to him in his prayers, and Carlo interprets this as divine accord with his decision. The crowd recognizes the statue he describes—it stands on a rock in Domrémy Forest. The king agrees to go there and meet his destiny, but is overwhelmed by the weight of crown and war.

Giacomo (Jacques) prowls near the same rock in Domrémy Forest, where his daughter, the shepherdess Giovanna (Joan), visits with suspicious frequency. He conceals himself as Giovanna descends from the Virgin's shrine deep in thought, praying that she might take up arms and fly to battle, soon falling asleep. Carlo arrives, apprehensive, and kneels in prayer, laying down his arms as he had in his vision. Giovanna's simultaneous dream is visited by demons, then by angels who herald her the chosen saviour of the French. She starts up—"I am ready!"—and, immediately recognizing the Dauphin, collects his armor and reveals to him her calling. Her missionary enthusiasm catches up Carlo, with whom she hastens away, but not Giacomo, who is convinced that devils have possessed his daughter.

ACT I. The English are amazed at the resilience of the French army, which has now taken the upper hand in the fighting. In his grieving encampment, the English commander, Talbot, receives the disheveled Giacomo, who says he can capture for the English the maid who has wrought their destruction. He is still determined that Giovanna is empowered by forces of evil, and though he loves his country, he cannot abide its "dishonorable" victories. The English accept his offer.

Before Carlo's coronation, Giovanna is remembering the simple happiness of her forest home. She decides to leave the cause and return, but Carlo begs her to stay and offers her his love. Just as she admits she loves him in return, Giovanna's voices warn her never to harbor worldly love in her heart. She draws back, seeing her father's image pointing at her and calling for her death. Carlo calms her, but not enough to conceal her agitation from the officers calling them to the coronation. A chorus of demons chides Giovanna as she leaves with the Dauphin.

ACT II. In the great square of Rheims, Giacomo watches the procession from the crowd, which extols Giovanna in particular. When she comes out of the church with the king, Giacomo steps forward and imprecates his daughter before all. The mob is inclined to believe the story, especially when the speechless Giovanna offers no words in her own defense. Utterly confused, she bursts into tears and falls into her father's arms. Carlo is shocked by the fickleness of the people, who cheer Giacomo's suggestion that the witch be burned.

ACT III.   Imprisoned by the English, Giovanna is awakened by battle cries. She experiences great frustration when her chains keep her from participating. Giacomo overhears her urging her countrymen on and begins to realize his mistake. After he frees her, he observes her progress in battle from a promontory—she saves the king, routs the English and takes their stronghold. Rejoicing is cut short when Giovanna, mortally wounded, is carried in on a litter. Miraculously she rises up, asking for the standard she always carried with her in battle so that she might restore it to heaven. Giovanna's angel voices call her heavenward and she sinks to the ground, bathed in a celestial light.

ALZIRA

PROLOGUE. THE PRISONER.   Mid-sixteenth-century Peru. A glorious sunrise illuminates the plains of the Rima valley. The Incas, led by Otumbo, drag in the captive Alvaro, Spanish governor of Peru, tie him to a tree and dance threateningly around him. Alvaro's Christian prayers are met with the whoops of his vengeful captors. The warrior Zamoro arrives in a canoe. As chief of the tribe, he pardons Alvaro and sends him back to Lima, telling him to spread word of his beneficent barbarian liberator. Otumbo reveals that Alzira, Zamoro's intended, has been taken by the enemy with her father. This and his hatred of oppression inspire Zamoro to a battle cry; the Incas embark on a mission of rescue and revenge.

ACT I. A LIFE FOR A LIFE.   Martial strains bring Alvaro before a crowd of Spanish officers in Lima's central square. He abdicates his governorship to his son Gusmano, whose inaugural act is to declare peace with the Incas, publicly recognizing Ataliba, Alzira's father, whom he asks for his daughter's hand, to placate his love and draw Incas and Spaniards closer together.

In her father's apartments in the governor's palace, the sleeping Alzira is watched over by her sister Zuma. Alzira is awakened by a disturbing dream in which she was saved from drowning by her beloved Zamoro, whom she believes to have perished on the battlefield. She rejects her father's command that she marry the murderer of her betrothed and arrogator of her people's lands and rights. Alzira's next visitor is actually Zamoro, with whom she enjoys a tender reunion. Returning with Gusmano, Ataliba is confronted with the embracing lovers. When the fuming Gusmano promises terrible tortures for Zamoro, the Incan retorts that for all his talk, Gusmano has never dared to fight him. Alvaro appears and requests clemency for the man who once saved his life, but Gusmano is unrelenting until a Spanish captain brings word that the Incan tribesmen are marching on Lima calling for their leader. Now Gusmano hears his father and spares a life for a life, though he spits abuse at Zamoro when the latter vows to scalp him in the fray.

ACT II. THE VENGEANCE OF A SAVAGE. The Incas have lost the battle and among the prisoners dragged into the Spanish fort is Zamoro, whose life Gusmano will spare only if Alzira consents to accept his troth. This she does after pleading at length with the despot, and Zamoro is saved from the stake.

Zamoro, costumed as a Spanish soldier, arrives at a cave where Incan survivors of the battle have been hiding. Wasted with grief, the warrior hates life without Alzira. When Otumbo confirms that she has wed Gusmano, Zamoro's frantic woe turns to anger, thence to revenge.

In the fortress at Lima, the wedding festivities are in full swing. Gusmano addresses the party, full of love for Alzira and happy in victory, but when he reaches for the hand of his mortified bride, he is stabbed by Zamoro, still disguised as a soldier. Ennobled by imminent death, the governor sheds his pride in a generous decree: Zamoro is to be pardoned and given the hand of his faithful love. Gusmano dies in his father's arms.

ATTILA

PROLOGUE. The city of Aquileia is smoldering in the wake of Attila's invasion (c. 454); the ruthless Hun has swept all before him in his conquest of Italy. In a square, Huns, Herulians and Ostrogoths celebrate the occupation and prostrate themselves before Attila when his chariot appears, hailing him as Odin's earthly envoy. The conquerer is impressed by a group of Aquileian warrior maidens, saved from the purge by his slave Uldino for their bravery. He is especially taken with Odabella (daughter of the slain lord of Aquileia), who stands forth and exalts the courage of Italian women who stand and fight for their country—not sitting and weeping like the barbarians' women. When Attila, weakened, gives her his sword, she blesses her hour of vengeance. The women depart and Attila welcomes his adversary, the Roman general Ezio, whose excellence in war the Hun admires. Ezio has private business: he offers to join with Attila in overthrowing the old, weak ruler of Constantinople to the east and Valentinian, the youth who rules to the west. Then Ezio will leave the world for Attila, claiming only Italy for himself. Attila refuses the Roman and asserts that all Italy, including Rome itself, will know Odin's wrath. Ezio stalks out angrily.

Before dawn on the mudflats of the Adriatic lagoons, a chorus of hermits huddles from a storm. As the waters grow calm, hundreds of boats are seen, bearing Aquileian refugees in their direction. Upon landing, their leader, Foresto, bids them settle in, then abhorring the bondage of his beloved Odabella to Attila. The refugees determine that a phoenix will rise—they will build a city on that spot.

ACT I.   Alone near Attila's camp, Odabella weeps openly for her father and betrothed, whom she presumes dead. But he soon surprises her by appearing disguised as a barbarian. He resents the dangers he braved to come to her, upbraiding her for her complaisance in the hands of the enemy. Hurt, Odabella disabuses her lover of this notion saying that, like the Biblical Judith, she will wreak a bloody vengeance on her enemy's leader. She proposes Attila's own sword as her weapon.

That same night, Attila is awakened in his tent by a nightmare in which a great, aged man halted his advance on Rome, calling him a scourge against mankind and barring him from despoiling Christian soil. Attila is now doubly determined to destroy Rome and rallies his men. On the march, their songs to Odin are diffused by the strains of Christian hymns. A procession approaches, headed by the same elder as in Attila's dream—Leo, Bishop of Rome. When he speaks the very words Attila heard in his dream, the Hun cowers, terrified by a vision of Saints Peter and Paul holding him at bay with flaming swords. The invaders are shocked, while the Christians praise God.

ACT II.   In his camp, Ezio broods over a letter from Valentinian recalling him to Rome: he senses the young emperor fears him more than Attila, with whom he has signed a truce. Ezio's soliloquy on the decline of Roman glory is interrupted by a group of Attila's slaves inviting Ezio to a feast in the enemy camp. One remains behind; it is Foresto, who reveals that a mountainside fire will signal the Roman troops to fall on the Huns.

As the Romans arrive, some Druids warn Attila not to sit at table with old enemies; he overlooks the suggestion and orders a dance. Foresto tells Odabella that Attila's cup is poisoned. To save vengeance for herself, Odabella stays Attila's hand as he makes to drink. When the Hun demands to know the author of this treason, Foresto steps forward. But Odabella claims her lover's life as her reward for saving Attila, though Foresto reviles her.

ACT III.   Attila has claimed Odabella as his queen, and Foresto lies in wait with Ezio to ambush the wedding party. But the agitated Odabella rushes in, pleading forgiveness from her father's ghost for marrying his victor. Foresto confronts her, but she insists she loves him. Attila arrives looking for his bride and accuses all three of underhanded treachery. Odabella stabs him with his own sword and embraces Foresto as Roman soldiers hail the final avenging.

MACBETH

ACT I.   Scotland, 1040. Macbeth and Banquo, generals in the army of King Duncan of Scotland, meet three witches while crossing a desolate heath. These hags prophetically hail Macbeth as Thane of Cawdor and future king, Banquo as father of kings thereafter; no sooner have they vanished than messengers from Duncan approach, proclaiming Macbeth the new Thane of Cawdor. Amazed at this turn of events, Macbeth hesitates to ponder the gaining of the crown.

In the hall of her castle, Lady Macbeth reads a letter from her husband describing his meeting with the witches. Exulting in the prospect of power, she vows to add her own cunning and boldness to Macbeth's ambition. When a servant brings word that the king will spend the night in the castle, she calls on the ministers of hell to inspire her wicked plans. Macbeth enters and his wife persuades him to murder Duncan that very night. Just then Duncan and his train arrive; they retire at once. Macbeth, dreading his task, imagines a bloody dagger before his eyes, but as the signal bell sounds, he steals into the royal bedchamber. Lady Macbeth reenters a moment before her husband staggers horrified from the room to tell her the deed is done. Seeing the dagger still in his hands, she cold-bloodedly takes the weapon from him and goes to smear blood on the royal guards, who have been drugged. There is a knock at the gate; when Lady Macbeth returns, the couple withdraw. The nobleman Macduff enters with Banquo; they soon discover the murder and immediately summon the entire court, which invokes God's vengeance.

ACT II. Not satisfied with their uneasy throne, Macbeth and his wife plot the murder of Banquo and his son, lest the latter one day gain the crown as the witches prophesied. After her husband hurries off, Lady Macbeth reaffirms their faith in the knife, glorying in her royal rank.

A group of assassins await Banquo in a deserted park. Troubled by a foreboding of evil, he is set upon and killed, but his son Fleance escapes.

In the banquet hall, Lady Macbeth toasts her guests in a brilliant drinking song while Macbeth, secretly informed that the murder has been done, complains to the assembly of Banquo's absence. Suddenly, to the guests' astonishment, he imagines he can see the general's ghost seated at the table. Lady Macbeth scolds her husband fiercely and he momentarily regains his calm as she sings a reprise of the drinking song. But when the bloody specter continues to haunt him, the guests comment on his strange behavior and his decomposing realm.

ACT III. In an eerie cave, the witches stir their caldron. A haggard Macbeth enters to learn his fate, and at his insistence they conjure up a series of apparitions. The first, a warrior's head, tells him to beware Macduff; the second, a bloody child, assures him that no man born of woman can harm him; finally, a crowned child reveals that he will rule invincible till Birnam Wood marches against him. Somewhat reassured, he asks the witches if Banquo's sons will ever reign in Scotland; in reply they invoke the spirits of eight kings, who pass before the terrified Macbeth. The last of the line is Banquo, holding a mirror that reflects the other kings. As Macbeth faints in dread, the witches disappear. Lady Macbeth enters, and the enraged couple vow to uphold their reign of blood and kill all who oppose them.

ACT IV. Near Birnam Wood a band of Scottish refugees bewail their oppressed homeland, caught in the gory grip of Macbeth's tyranny. Macduff, grieving over his murdered wife and children, is joined by Duncan's son Malcolm; they instruct their soldiers to cut branches from the forest as camouflage for an attack on Macbeth's castle. The two leaders unite with the crowd in a call to arms.

A physician and lady-in-waiting observe the guilt-wracked and exhausted Lady Macbeth as she wanders in her sleep, wiping imaginary bloodstains from her hands.

On a battlefield near the castle, Macbeth clings to the hope that he can withstand the forces of Malcolm and Macduff, but he is soul-weary and curses his fate. Word of his wife's death reaches him just as messengers bring the astounding news that Birnam Wood is advancing toward him; Macbeth leads his men to battle, seeking death or victory. Macduff seeks out Macbeth and, crying that he was not born of woman but torn prematurely from his mother's womb, fells the king with his sword. Dying, Macbeth curses the day he heeded the witches' prophecies. Macduff's soldiers hail Malcolm as the new king.

I MASNADIERI

ACT I. Early 1700's. Carlo, favorite son of the old Count Massimiliano Moor, is reading in a Saxon tavern, daydreaming about his beloved home and sweetheart, Amalia. His envious younger brother, Francesco, knowing that Carlo has fallen in with a decadent set at the university, has poisoned his reputation at home and sent him a letter of rejection in his father's name, all to clear inheritance and title for himself. Carlo expects the letter contains his pardon, and is so furious upon reading it that he espouses his friends' suggestion that they form a band of outlaws with him as leader. They recklessly pledge their lives and fates.

At home, Francesco ruminates on a new obstacle: to rid himself of his father, he has his steward, Arminio, disguise himself as Carlo's comrade and announce to Massimiliano that Carlo died in battle in Prague, seeking release from parental repudiation. The two find the old man in his bedroom, where Amalia watches over his fitful sleep. Arminio tells his tale, with Francesco feigning concern for Massimiliano's reaction, and produces the sword that "killed" Carlo. On it, written in blood, are words absolving Amalia from her marriage vow and encouraging her to wed Francesco. Massimiliano is undone, and as Francesco hoped, he collapses and is pronounced dead by Amalia.

ACT II.   Amalia, grieving by Massimiliano's tomb, pauses when the guilty Arminio steals by to tell her that both Carlo and the old man are alive. When Francesco appears, ardent with nuptial promises, Amalia spurns him, though without revealing what she knows. He threatens her with violence, but she snatches his dagger and holds him off.

In a Bohemian wood, Carlo is hailed by his bandits, who extol his daring in saving a companion from hanging and setting fire to Prague. But Carlo is depressed thinking of his home and his love. Surrounded, the band melts into the forest to put the pursuers to rout.

Amalia has escaped Francesco and hides in a wood, where Carlo and his company have also sought refuge. By chance, the lovers are happily reunited, but Carlo cannot bring himself to reveal to Amalia his connection with robbers. Returning to camp, the shamed Carlo considers suicide. Nearby, Arminio comes to a dungeon with food and is caught by Carlo, who finds the desiccated figure behind the bars is none other than his father, left to die but kept alive by Arminio's provisions. When the father relates how Francesco buried him alive knowingly, Carlo, still incognito, rallies his bandits in a frenzy of revenge.

ACT III.   Francesco awakes from a vivid dream of the dead rising against him and severe punishment from God. The priest he summons allows him no absolution, citing the two crimes most offensive to the Lord: parricide and fratricide. In a fury, Francesco breaks off praying—"Hell will not deride *me*!"

While Carlo's men track Francesco, Massimiliano expresses his wish to forgive his evil son; Carlo asks for his blessing from the old man and thanks God when returning outlaws say that they failed to capture his brother. Now Amalia arrives and runs into Carlo's arms and he is forced to divulge his identity as bandit chief to father and sweetheart, a confession that thoroughly humiliates him. Despite the enthusiastic pardon from both Massimiliano and Amalia, Carlo is claimed by the bandits, who remind him of his oaths. Doubly disgraced, Carlo complies with Amalia's cry for death: stabbing her, he rushes out—"to the gallows."

JERUSALEM

Jérusalem is a relatively faithful adaptation of *I Lombardi alla Prima Crociata*. Its triumphant crusaders are French rather than Italian, but they fight at the same time as do Verdi's earlier Lombards—the period of the First Crusade.

ACT I.   Hélène, the daughter of Count Raymond of Toulouse, concludes a rendezvous with Gaston, Viscount of Béarn, who will forget his feud with the Count if Hélène and Gaston may marry. Hélène prays with her friend Isaure for Gaston's safety. The palace hall fills to hear the Count bless his daughter's union with the Viscount. Only Roger, the Count's brother, is displeased, for he adores Hélène. He broods elsewhere as a Papal emissary appoints the Count leader of the French Crusade. The Count gives his white cape to Gaston as a symbol of bonded friendship. Later, when Roger hires a soldier to murder Gaston, he instructs the man to kill not the knight in white, but the man next to him, thinking that will be Gaston. Noise breaks out in the chapel and Roger is aghast when the Viscount emerges in one piece. The hired killer has stabbed the Count and been caught; Roger whispers to him that they must save each other. The soldier thinks to accuse Gaston, and the crowd falls for this trick, not surprised that the Viscount should reopen the feud at close range. When they have cornered the innocent Gaston, the official from Rome brings down an anathema on him, refusing him Christian charity and exiling him. The wounded Count is meanwhile removed on a litter.

ACT II.   Near Palestine, a white-haired hermit (Roger) prays before the cross outside his mountain cave; his ambition is to expiate his sins by saving the Holy Sepulchre from the Moslems. Hélène and Isaure appear while Roger is administering to thirsting pilgrims on the hill. Convinced that Gaston is both innocent and alive, Hélène is happy to discover the Viscount's squire among the pilgrims; he assures her that her beloved is a living prisoner of the Emir of Ramla. Hélène goes off, determined to find and free her love. Leading the crusaders who now arrive is the fully recovered Count of Toulouse, who asks the hermit for his blessing. Moved, the hermit responds by asking if he might join the fight. Finally, the entire assembly marches off toward Ramla.

The Emir, who has kept Gaston alive so as not to incur the wrath of the Christians, is now anxious to divine the identity of a disguised maiden arrested in Ramla. Hélène is brought in. Her reaction at seeing Gaston is noted by the Emir, who leaves them alone, but observed. They fall into

139

each other's arms and make to escape to the crusaders visible in the valley, but are surrounded and detained.

ACT III.   Hélène, enveloped by a sarcastic corps of dancing odalisques, is confined to the harem, where the Emir appears to admonish her that if the crusaders storm his city, their leader will be presented with his own daughter's head. Soon enough, the Christians do arrive, scattering all before them. The Count repudiates his daughter for consorting with the man who tried to take his life, drags her off and enchains Gaston, who had come to rescue Hélène from harm.

Gaston is humiliated and condemned anew in a square in Ramla, enduring unspeakable abuse in spite of his honest attempts to convince his accusers of his innocence. The execution is set for the next day.

ACT IV.   In the Valley of Jehoshaphat, the hermit, now widely respected as a holy man, is called upon by the Pope's envoy to grant absolution to the condemned Gaston. Roger gives his sword to the man accused of his own crimes in order that he may rescue the Holy Sepulchre. The sound of fighting draws them off into the fray.

Hélène and Isaure witness the triumphal procession returning to the camp. The most valorous knight, it turns out, is Gaston, who appeals for justice. But Roger stumbles in, fatally wounded, confesses his crimes and his identity, thereby truly absolving Gaston at last. He asks for a final view of reclaimed Jerusalem and dies.

IL CORSARO

ACT I.   The beginning of the nineteenth century. Corrado is cheered up by his fellow corsairs on their island in the Aegean; he is unhappy to be an outcast, as indeed they all are, and furthermore suggests that unluck in first love turned him against mankind. When his companion delivers a message from a Greek spy, Corrado calls the pirates to ship and arms.

His beloved, Medora, awaits Corrado's return in her tower by the sea. Inclined to think the worst, she laments, accompanying herself on a harp. She is elated when Corrado appears, in mid-journey, just to see her. Soon he is summoned by a booming cannon and, acknowledging Medora's anguished protestations of grief, swears to return to her. She swoons as he rushes away.

ACT II. Over Coron harbor, odalisques in Pasha Seid's harem adorn Gulnara, his favorite, but she asserts that all his riches will not win her love. A eunuch invites her to the feast, where Seid will celebrate his victory in advance. Gulnara hopes that heaven will grant her return to her homeland.

Seid receives guests in a shoreside pavilion, promising success to warriors who fight in Allah's name. A dervish is announced—it is Corrado pretending that he has escaped the corsairs. Presently the scene is illumined by a fire in the harbor. Throwing off his disguise, Corrado signals his pirates, who overrun the scene. Corrado decides to save the women heard crying from the harem, but his chivalry proves fatal: the delay gives the Turks the edge and many of his men are captured. Corrado defies his captor, scorning death and declaring revenge, while the women implore Seid's mercy. But the Pasha plans a slow, agonizing death for the corsair.

ACT III. Later, Seid voices his suspicions that Gulnara, the one woman he has really loved, is enamored of Corrado. Gulnara comes to his apartments, suggesting he spare Corrado and collect a fabulous ransom. This ruse to keep Corrado alive Seid figures out immediately, and he tells Gulnara she loves in vain. Outraged, she mutters a vendetta.

The spirited Corrado is restless in his cell chains, thinking about death, honor and Medora. Gulnara enters, having arranged for his escape, but he will not go, convinced that heaven has spoken his fate. Dagger in hand, Gulnara exits hurriedly, soon returning: she has killed Pasha Seid in his sleep. Corrado is persuaded and the two escape to a waiting ship.

Convinced that her love is no more, the melancholy Medora prepares for death. She has already poisoned herself when a ship is sighted. It carries Corrado to her, but too late. She dies in his arms. He, disconsolate, hurls himself into the sea, while the compassionate Gulnara falls senseless.

LA BATTAGLIA DI LEGNANO

ACT I. HE LIVES! It is 1176. By the gates of Milan, soldiers from all the Lombard cities gather while an enthusiastic crowd breaks out in the song of the Lombard League, which has been organized to chase Federico Barbarossa, German invader, out of Italy. The leader from Verona steps forward, praising the city of Milan. This is Arrigo, whose appearance confounds the Milanese captain Rolando, an old friend who had left him for dead at the Siege of Susa, and who now greets him tenderly. Both respond splendidly to a consular exhortation of allegiance, leading an oath pledging their lives to Italy's defense.

In a grove on Rolando's properties, his wife, Lida, cannot join in the rejoicing, for this war has deprived her of her parents and brother; her tears would lead to death were it not for her child. Marcovaldo, a German prisoner set free by Rolando, futilely presses his attentions on Lida. When her confidante, Imelda, brings news that Rolando is returning with Arrigo—to whom Lida was once engaged—Lida's joy that he lives does not escape Marcovaldo's notice. Rolando happily presents his wife to Arrigo, who cringes. An old wound, he says, bothers him. But when he is left alone with Lida, Arrigo betrays his real reason for hurt: he is outraged that Lida has defiled her promise of eternal fidelity to him by marrying. Despite Lida's explanation that she thought him dead and was encouraged to marry Rolando by her father, the embittered Arrigo stalks out, leaving her despondent.

ACT II. BARBAROSSA.   In the city hall at Como, dukes and magistrates collect furtively to receive members of the Lombard League (led by Rolando and Arrigo), who repudiate the weak Comaschi for signing a treaty with Barbarossa, averring that though Italians in fact, the rulers of Como are barbarians at heart. But Como will not join the League. When Arrigo asks what he should reply to the League, Barbarossa himself appears with an answer: shutters are opened to expose a formidable display of German military might on the hillside. But Arrigo and Rolando know that these mercenaries can never defeat a people fighting for their own freedom. Italy's destiny will never change. "*I* am Italy's destiny!" cries Barbarossa grandly.

ACT III. THE DISGRACE.   In a crypt in the basilica of St. Ambrose, Arrigo comes to enlist with the Knights of Death, who swear to rid Italy of the Germans or die in the attempt. Impressed by Arrigo's determination, their leader abdicates his position to the warrior.

Lida, now convinced that her lack of faith has driven Arrigo to this death vow, speeds him a letter through Imelda. Rolando, off to battle, blesses wife and child and takes leave of Arrigo, to whom he entrusts the care of Milan during his surprise campaign against Barbarossa. Indeed, if he should fall, Arrigo is to assume the care of his family as well. Marcovaldo, who has intercepted Lida's note to her lover, shows it to Rolando when Arrigo goes off as proof of his wife's infidelity. Furious, Rolando resolves to set matters straight.

A pensive Arrigo comes in from his balcony and writes a letter to his mother. Lida enters quietly. She admits to loving Arrigo, but feels they must remain apart, he for his mother's sake, she for her duty to her little boy. When Rolando knocks to call Arrigo to the Knights of Death, Lida conceals herself out on the balcony. Arrigo claims it is still too dark to leave, but Rolando proves him wrong by pulling open the shutters. There stands Lida. Deciding to let infamy be their punishment, Rolando locks the lovers into the room. Arrigo cannot resist the call to arms from without and leaps to the moat below to join his fellow soldiers.

ACT IV. TO DIE FOR ONE'S COUNTRY. A crowd mills before a church in Milan, waiting for word of the League. Lida and Imelda join the general prayer. A consul affirms that the Lombards have defeated the Germans and that Arrigo of Verona dispatched Barbarossa personally. The celebration cools when a funeral cortege advances. The Knights of Death bear in Arrigo, whose last breath is spent assuring Rolando that Lida is without guilt. "He who dies for his country cannot be evil in his soul," asserts the assembly as husband and wife are reconciled and Rolando embraces his dying friend. The strains of a Te Deum filter from the church; Arrigo kisses the flag of the fatherland and dies in peace.

LUISA MILLER

ACT I. LOVE. The inhabitants of an eighteenth-century Tyrolean village greet Luisa Miller on her birthday. Embraced by her father, she looks around for her beloved, a young hunter who calls himself Carlo—though he is in fact Rodolfo, the local count's son. Luisa joyously recalls their first meeting. When Rodolfo enters, the lovers proclaim undying fidelity while Miller voices concern lest the young man seduce his daughter. As the others leave for church, Wurm, the Count's retainer, demands Luisa's hand in marriage for himself, calling on Miller to honor an earlier promise. But Miller refuses to force his daughter's consent, whereupon Wurm reveals Rodolfo's identity; Miller's fears for Luisa increase.

In Count Walter's castle, Wurm tells his master of Rodolfo's love for Luisa. Enraged at his son's audacity in wooing a village girl, the Count dismisses Wurm and decries the lot of fatherhood. When his son enters, the Count reveals that he has promised Rodolfo to his cousin, Federica, Duchess of Ostheim, and insists that his son formally ask for her hand. Federica arrives, and the Count leaves the young couple alone. Though Rodolfo tells Federica, who has worshiped him since childhood, that he loves another, she jealously refuses to break their engagement.

At home, Miller tells Luisa that Rodolfo has lied and is about to contract a wealthy marriage. He swears vengeance on the youth for trifling with his daughter under false pretenses. Overhearing Miller as he arrives, Rodolfo swears he intends to marry Luisa; he can force his father's approval, he says, because he knows the secret of how the Count gained his title (by murdering his cousin). Seconds later, Count Walter himself appears and brands Luisa a scheming seductress. Miller indignantly threatens the Count, who calls his men to arrest father and daughter. Ignoring Luisa's pleas and the wrath of Miller and Rodolfo, the Count frees the prisoners only when Rodolfo threatens to divulge his secret.

ACT II. INTRIGUE.   In Miller's house, villagers tell Luisa her father has been kidnaped. Wurm appears, dismisses the others and informs Luisa that she can forestall her father's execution only if she writes a letter addressed to Wurm, admitting she sought Rodolfo for his wealth and pledging herself to Wurm. Praying for help, she writes the letter, only to hear she must accompany Wurm to the castle to display her love for him. Cursing him, she agrees.

In the castle, Count Walter awaits Wurm, who soon enters to tell him the letter is written. The two men plot to send it to Rodolfo. Recalling the murder he committed, with Wurm's help, to gain his position, the Count says his son knows of the deed; the frightened Wurm leaves to fetch Luisa as Federica approaches. Luisa, with Wurm and Walter goading her on with threats against her father, professes to the overjoyed Federica her love for Wurm, denying that she ever loved Rodolfo.

In the courtyard, Rodolfo reads Luisa's letter, recalls their love and believes himself betrayed. He summons Wurm for a duel, but the cowardly retainer fires into the air, bringing the Count and a crowd of soldiers. Count Walter, feigning concern, suggests marriage to Federica as the only revenge for Luisa's treachery. Rodolfo abandons all hope and agrees.

ACT III. POISON.   Surrounded by friends, Luisa sadly welcomes her father home after he is set free. Alone with his daughter, he pleads with her not to take her own life; they will leave the village together the next morning. Miller departs, and as an organ is heard in the neighboring church, Luisa kneels to pray. Quietly, Rodolfo enters holding Luisa's false letter. He pours poison from a phial into a cup. When Luisa admits to having written the letter to Wurm, he asks for a drink, as if ill, and Luisa gives him the poisoned cup; he then offers it to her, and she, too, drinks. Trying to comfort him, she never dreams his words portend death. When he tells her the cup is poisoned, Luisa confesses her letter was a lie to free her father. Miller himself appears, only to have Luisa ask for his blessing and then die in his arms. Wurm and the Count now arrive. With his last breath Rodolfo kills Wurm, as Miller and the Count stand horrified at the death of their children.

STIFFELIO

ACT I.   Early nineteenth-century Germany. Some years before the action begins, a man called Müller, the leader of a persecuted German Protestant sect (the Assassverians), had been taken in by the elderly Count Stankar, one of his followers. Under the name Stiffelio, Müller found further refuge in the Count's daughter Lina, whom he wed. But affairs of faith have required him to travel often and long. During his latest absence, Lina has commenced an affair with Raffaele, a handsome young nobleman friendly with her cousin Federico. The minister Jorg sits reading Klopstock's *Messias* as the curtain rises, waiting for Stiffelio's return. Upon arrival, Stiffelio, warmly welcomed by Count Stankar, says a boatman saw a youth appear at a castle window at dawn and dive into the waves below, encouraged by an anxious woman. Lina and Raffaele, present in the company, realize they have been seen. Stankar's suspicions of an affair are meanwhile confirmed, and he resolves to watch over Lina for the sake of his family honor, while Stiffelio destroys the evidence—the diver's wallet —before opening it. Stiffelio, glad to be alone with his wife, feels relief in finding her fidelity at the end of his journey, which revealed to him the horrors of greed and conjugal sin. Lina almost confesses her transgression, especially when Stiffelio asks why she isn't wearing their ring. Stankar interrupts—the guests are waiting. Raffaele sneaks in when they go and leaves a letter for Lina in a book, surreptitiously observed by Jorg. Federico comes to fetch the book a few moments later. Now Lina returns to attempt a confession to Stiffelio in writing. Stankar, however, storms in and snatches up what she has written—"I am no longer worthy of you." He forces her to abandon the letter and conceal her illicit love, lest the affair disgrace the family.

At Stiffelio's reception in the great hall, Jorg discloses that he saw a young man hide a note in a book but could not distinguish his identity. Stiffelio grabs the book from Federico, whom he suspects, and breaks the lock. Stankar picks up the letter that falls out and tears it to pieces before Stiffelio can read it, but in an aside he challenges Raffaele to a duel.

ACT II. Raffaele comes to the graveyard, where Lina is praying at her mother's tomb. He refuses to give her back the ring she gave him. Suddenly Stankar appears with two swords and, goading Raffaele on with insults, arouses him to duel. Lina flees, but their fighting brings on Stiffelio, who calls them off and takes Raffaele's hand affectionately. Stankar blurts out that the man whose hand Stiffelio holds is his betrayer. Lina reenters, Stiffelio comprehends and, seizing Stankar's sword, challenges Raffaele, who refuses to fight a priest. The congregation is heard within the church, asking the Lord for mercy; Jorg arrives to extend this sentiment to Stiffelio, who collapses on the church steps, torn between his aristocratic breeding, which demands revenge, and his Christian ethics, which demand forgiveness.

ACT III. Alone in the castle, Stankar sorts out his quandary, lamenting his dishonorable daughter. When Jorg announces that the lovers have not fled, the old Count departs with plans to challenge Raffaele again. The latter arrives now with Stiffelio, who leaves him in an adjoining room while confronting Lina with divorce documents, which will allow him to turn to religion and Lina to follow her heart. As she claims to have loved Stiffelio always, and to have been betrayed by Raffaele, Stankar staggers in. He has dispatched Raffaele and cleansed the family name. Jorg calls them all to church for prayer.

ACT IV. Stiffelio, nearly delirious, mounts the pulpit to deliver his sermon. His Bible falls open to John 8, and he reads Christ's words about the adulterous woman: "Let he that is without sin among you cast the first stone." Addressing Lina, who kneels below him, Stiffelio continues, "And the woman . . . the woman rose, pardoned."

RIGOLETTO

ACT I. Sixteenth-century. Strolling among the courtiers in his palace ballroom, the Duke of Mantua lightheartedly boasts of his way with women.

After dancing with his newest quarry, Countess Ceprano, he escorts her from the room, followed by his hunchbacked jester, Rigoletto, who openly mocks the Countess' enraged but helpless husband. A courtier, Marullo, spreads the latest gossip: Rigoletto is suspected of keeping a young mistress in his home. The jester returns with the Duke and, sure of his master's protection, continues to taunt Ceprano, who plots with the others to punish him. When Monterone, an elderly nobleman, forces his way into the room to denounce the Duke for seducing his daughter, he is viciously derided by Rigoletto. As Monterone is arrested, he pronounces a father's curse on the Duke and the jester, who falls to the floor in terror.

Late that night, brooding over Monterone's curse, Rigoletto hurries to the house where he has hidden his daughter, Gilda. On the way he encounters Sparafucile, a professional assassin, who offers his services; but the jester dismisses him, reflecting that his own tongue is as sharp as the murderer's dagger. His mood brightens when he is greeted by Gilda, who questions him about her long-dead mother; Rigoletto fondly recalls his wife—now Gilda is all he has left. Afraid for the girl's safety, he warns her nurse, Giovanna, to admit no one to the house. As the jester leaves, however, the Duke slips into the garden, tossing a purse to Giovanna to keep her quiet. He declares his love to Gilda, who has secretly admired him at church, and tells her he is Gualtier Maldé, a poor student. At the sound of footsteps Gilda begs him to leave; alone, she tenderly repeats his name and retires. Meanwhile, the malicious courtiers stop Rigoletto outside his house and ask him to help abduct Ceprano's wife, who lives nearby. The jester is duped into wearing a blindfold and holding a ladder against his own garden wall. Laughing at how they have tricked him, the courtiers break into his house and carry off Gilda. Rigoletto, hearing his daughter's cry for help, tears off his blindfold and rushes into the house; discovering only her scarf, he remembers Monterone's curse.

ACT II.   In his palace, the Duke is distraught over the kidnapping of Gilda, whom he imagines alone and miserable. When his courtiers return, saying that it is they who have taken her and that she is now in his chamber, he rushes off to the conquest. Soon Rigoletto enters, searching for Gilda; though the courtiers are astonished to learn she is not his mistress but his daughter, they bar his way. The jester lashes out at their cruelty, but ends his tirade with a plea for mercy. Just then Gilda appears, disheveled in her nightdress. She runs in shame to her father, who orders the others to leave. Alone with Rigoletto, Gilda tells of the Duke's courtship, then of her abduction. As Monterone is led to the dungeons, still cursing the Duke, the jester swears vengeance while the lovelorn Gilda begs forgiveness for the Duke.

ACT III.   On a dark night, Rigoletto and Gilda wait outside the lonely inn on the outskirts of Mantua where Sparafucile and his sister Maddalena live. Gilda watches in disbelief while the Duke, disguised as a soldier and laughing at the fickleness of women, makes love to Maddalena. Telling Gilda to dress as a boy, the jester sends her off to Verona, then pays Sparafucile to murder the Duke, and leaves. As a storm gathers, Gilda returns to overhear Maddalena urge her brother to spare the handsome stranger and kill Rigoletto instead. Sparafucile refuses but agrees to substitute the next guest who comes to the inn. Gilda, resolved to sacrifice herself for the Duke even though he has betrayed her, knocks at the door and is stabbed. When the storm subsides, Rigoletto returns to claim the body; he gloats over the sack Sparafucile gives him, only to hear his supposed victim singing in the distance. Frantically cutting open the sack, he finds his daughter, who dies asking his forgiveness.

IL TROVATORE

ACT I. THE DUEL.   Outside the guardroom of Aliaferia Palace in Aragon,

Count di Luna's soldiers are waiting to apprehend a troubadour, in Manrico, who rivals the Count for the favors of the lady Leonora by serenading her after dark. Ferrando, captain of the guard, keeps his men awake by telling them of a gypsy woman burned at the stake years ago for bewitching Di Luna's younger brother. The gypsy's daughter sought vengeance by kidnaping the child and, so the story goes, burning him at the very stake where her mother died. Di Luna, though, still hopes his brother lives. As midnight tolls, the soldiers disperse.

In the palace gardens, Leonora confides to Inez how at a tournament she met an unknown knight in black armor and placed the victory wreath on his brow; she saw him no more until he came to serenade her. Though Inez expresses misgivings, Leonora declares her love for the handsome stranger. No sooner do the women reenter the palace than Di Luna arrives to court Leonora. Simultaneously, Manrico's song is heard in the distance and, rushing forth to greet him, Leonora finds both men in the garden. The jealous Count challenges Manrico to a duel.

ACT II. THE GYPSY. As dawn breaks in the Biscay mountains, a band of gypsies sing as they work with hammer and anvil. Azucena—the gypsy's daughter described by Ferrando—relives her mother's fiery execution, recalling her plea for vengeance. Manrico, weak from wounds sustained in battle, asks to hear her full story, becoming confused when Azucena, overwhelmed with memories, blurts out that by mistake she hurled her own son into the flames. Assuring him of a mother's love, Azucena makes Manrico swear revenge; he says a strange power stayed his hand when he could have killed Di Luna in the duel. A messenger brings news that Leonora, thinking Manrico dead, plans to enter a convent. Despite Azucena's entreaties, Manrico rushes away.

The amorous Di Luna, burning with passion for Leonora, waits by the cloister to kidnap her. When she enters with the nuns, he strides forward, only to be halted by Manrico, who suddenly appears with his men. As the forces struggle, the lovers escape.

ACT III. THE GYPSY'S SON.   Di Luna has pitched camp near the bastion of Castellor, where to his dismay Manrico has taken Leonora. After soldiers declaim their eagerness for victory, Ferrando leads in Azucena, who has been found loitering near the camp. The gypsy describes her poor, lonely life and says she is only searching for her son. Di Luna reveals his identity, at which Azucena recoils and is recognized by Ferrando as the supposed murderess of Di Luna's baby brother. The Count orders her burned at the stake.

Inside the castle, Manrico assures Leonora that her love makes him invincible and that Di Luna's army will be conquered. As the couple prepares to go to the wedding chapel, Manrico's friend Ruiz bursts in to say that Azucena has been seized and tied to a stake. Manrico, climbing up to an outlook, stares in horror at the pyre, which has already been lit. He runs to his mother's rescue.

ACT IV. THE TORTURE.   Ruiz brings Leonora to the foot of Manrico's prison tower, where she voices her undying love and prays for his release. Monks are heard intoning a doleful Miserere for the soul of the condemned, while Manrico sings farewell from the inside of the bastion. Leonora resolves to save him, and when Di Luna appears, she agrees to give herself to him to save her lover, but secretly swallows poison.

In their cell, Manrico comforts Azucena, who longs to return to their peaceful home in the mountains. No sooner does the old gypsy fall asleep than Leonora runs in to tell Manrico he is saved, urging him to flee, but he comprehends the price of his freedom and denounces her as the poison begins to take effect. He takes her in his arms as she dies. Di Luna, cheated of his prize, furiously sends Manrico to the executioner's block, while Azucena, rousing from sleep, staggers to the window in time to see the ax fall. In exultation she cries her mother is avenged: Di Luna has killed his brother.

LA TRAVIATA

ACT I. In her Paris mansion (c. 1850), the courtesan Violetta Valery welcomes party guests, including friends Flora Bervoix, the Marquis d'Obigny, Baron Douphol and Gastone, who introduces a new admirer, Alfredo Germont. This young man, having adored Violetta from afar, addresses her with a drinking song; she joins in the salute to pleasure. An orchestra is heard in the next room, but as guests move there to dance, Violetta suffers an attack of faintness and remains behind momentarily. Concerned, Alfredo come back, and since they are alone he confesses his love. At first Violetta protests that love is nothing to her but a means of livelihood. Something about the young man's sincerity touches her, however, and she sends him off with a promise to meet him the next day. After the guests have gone home, Violetta wonders if Alfredo could actually be the man to fulfill her in a real love affair. She decides she only wants freedom, though Alfredo's voice, heard from outside, still argues in favor of romance.

ACT II. Alfredo has persuaded Violetta and is living with her happily in a villa near Paris. When the maid, Annina, reveals that Violetta has pawned her jewels to keep the villa, Alfredo resolves to leave for the city and reclaim them at his own cost. Violetta comes looking for him and finds an invitation from Flora to a party that night. But Violetta has no intention of going back to her old life. A servant announces a gentleman, who turns out to be Alfredo's father. Though impressed by Violetta's bearing and gentility, he demands that she renounce his son: the scandal of Alfredo's affair with her has threatened his daughter's engagement. Crushed, Violetta says she cannot, but Germont gradually convinces her, embracing her as a father. Alone, the desolate woman sends an acceptance note to Flora and begins her farewell note to Alfredo. He enters suddenly, surprising her, and she can barely control herself. She reminds him of how deeply she loves him before rushing out. Now a servant hands Alfredo her farewell as Germont returns to console his son with memories of family life in Provence and assures him that his indiscretions will be forgiven him. But Alfredo, seeing Flora's invitation, suspects Violetta has thrown him over for a new lover. Furious, he determines to confront her at the party.

ACT III.   At her soiree, Flora learns from the Marquis that Violetta and Alfredo have split up, then cedes the floor to hired entertainers—a band of matadors and fortune-telling gypsies. Soon Alfredo strides in, making snide comments about love and gambling recklessly at cards. Violetta has arrived with the Baron Douphol, who challenges Alfredo to a game and loses a small fortune to him. Everyone goes in to supper, but Violetta has asked Alfredo to see her. Fearful of the Baron's anger, she wants Alfredo to leave, but he misunderstands her apprehension and demands that she admit she loves Douphol. She pretends she does with great reluctance. Now Alfredo calls in the others, denounces his former love and hurls his winnings at her to repay her for her services. Germont enters in time to witness this and he berates his son for his graceless behavior as the guests rebuke Alfredo. Douphol challenges him to a duel; Flora supports the weakened Violetta.

ACT IV.   In Violetta's bedroom, Dr. Grenvil tells Annina that her mistress has only hours to live: tuberculosis has claimed her. Alone, Violetta produces a letter from Germont telling that the Baron was wounded in his duel with Alfredo, who knows all and is now on his way to beg her pardon. But she senses it is too late. Paris is celebrating Mardi Gras, and after revelers pass outside, Annina rushes in to announce Alfredo. The lovers ecstatically plan to leave Paris forever, to escape the stifling round of parties and gossip. Germont enters with the doctor just before Violetta is seized with a last resurgence of strength. Crying out that she feels life returning, she wilts dead at her lover's feet.

LES VÊPRES SICILIENNES

ACT I. In Palermo's great square, about 1282, resentful Sicilians watch the soldiers of the French occupation carouse. Duchess Elena, mourning her brother, Frederick of Austria, executed by the French for treason, prays that she may exact vengeance. When a drunken French officer commands a song from her, Elena responds with a metaphorical one about a near shipwreck, a thinly veiled incitement to the oppressed Sicilians to cast off fear and come into their own that brings the crowd to boiling point. The Sicilians' attack is halted by the appearance of the French governor, Monforte, whose guards release the young patriot Arrigo, held on a treason charge. Monforte questions Arrigo about his background; Arrigo answers in a defiant tone—he never knew his father, his mother is dead. The general feels that Arrigo's bravado deserves him a place in the French regiment, hinting that the youth's ill-omened love for Elena will undo him, but Arrigo scorns Monforte and his offer, determined to pursue both Elena and insurrectionary glory.

ACT II. At the seashore, the patriot leader Procida lovingly greets his homeland upon returning from exile. He informs Elena and Arrigo that Spanish support is on its way provided Sicily rises against its oppressors. Procida leaves, emphasizing his reliance on Arrigo. Alone, Arrigo and Elena exchange words of love; she promises him her hand if he will avenge her brother's death. A messenger from Monforte brings an invitation to a ball to Arrigo, who refuses; soldiers lead him away. A large group of Sicilians enter now to celebrate their engagements, soon followed by a column of French troops. The French gladly adopt Procida's suggestion that they abduct some of the local girls, which enrages the Sicilians (as Procida had intended), who swear vengeance, doubly so when a barge passes, carrying their own women and the carefree French to the ball.

ACT III. In his study, Monforte rereads a letter from a woman he had seduced years before. Before dying, she wrote to him revealing that their son, brought up to hate his father, is none other than Arrigo. When the young man is shown in, Monforte tells him the truth, hoping for a reconciliation. Although Arrigo is torn, he sees his plans with Elena threatened and finally rejects his father, deploring his mother's fate.

In a brilliantly lit hall, the ball begins with a ballet depicting the progress of the seasons. Among the Sicilian conspirators who have crept in disguised are Elena and Procida, who pins the conspirators' ribbons on Arrigo. Confused by conflicting loyalties, Arrigo warns his father of an assassination plot against him, then actually shields him when the conspirators attack. Monforte arrests all except Arrigo, whom he proclaims his savior and upon whose treachery the others vow to avenge themselves.

ACT IV. Armed with an order from Monforte, Arrigo hesitates before visiting the prisoners. Elena reviles him, but is moved when Arrigo says that Monforte is his father. She welcomes him back to the cause, confesses her suffering in hating him and pledges her deathless love. Soldiers bring on Procida, who tells Elena that an Aragonese ship laden with weapons lies off port. His suspicions are kindled when he notices Arrigo; he despairs when Monforte arrives with a mass death sentence and Arrigo is identified as the general's son. Monforte will not grant Arrigo's plea for clemency unless the youth recognizes his father. Weakened by the echo of the chanting monks and the sight of the execution block, Arrigo agrees. True to his promise, Monforte pardons everyone and consecrates the tie between his son and Elena to bring the rival peoples together.

ACT V.   By the chapel of Monforte's palace, knights and maidens admire Elena as she approaches, radiant in her bridal array. Arrigo joins her briefly before Procida announces to her that her wedding bells are the signal for the Sicilians to attack the unarmed French. Elena is horrified: she cannot denounce her friends any more than she can see her husband murdered. Eventually, she refuses to go through with the marriage. But Monforte brushes aside her refusal, convinced that she loves Arrigo. When the bells ring out, the shouts heard are not those of a joyous populace— rather, the bloodthirsty cries of vengeful Sicilians, who inundate the scene and fall upon Monforte and the French.

SIMON BOCCANEGRA

PROLOGUE.   In a public square of fourteenth-century Genoa, Paolo and Pietro, leaders of the People's Party, conspire to gain power over the aristocracy by electing a popular corsair, Simon Boccanegra, as doge. Their proposal is accepted by Boccanegra because the office would make possible his marriage to Maria Fiesco, who has been kept prisoner by her father, Jacopo Fiesco since she bore Boccanegra's daughter. A mob of commoners, incited by Pietro and Paolo, pledges support to the corsair. No sooner do they leave than Fiesco steps from his palace mourning Maria's death. Boccanegra returns and, unaware of the tragedy, seeks peace with Fiesco; the old man, however, demands that he first be given his granddaughter—only to learn from Simon that the child has disappeared.

Fiesco wrathfully withdraws, permitting Boccanegra to enter the palace and discover for himself Maria's casket. As he staggers back into the square, a crowd hails him as doge.

ACT I. Twenty-five years have passed. In the Grimaldi palace gardens, Amelia (Boccanegra's long-lost daughter) awaits her lover, Gabriele Adorno. When he arrives, she expresses her fear for their safety in the war between the Genoan patricians and plebeians. Gabriele, learning that the doge plans to give her in marriage to Paolo, obtains for himself the blessing of Amelia's guardian, Andrea (a pseudonym of the fugitive Fiesco, who does not realize that his ward is his granddaughter). The two men, determined to overthrow the doge, depart as a fanfare announces Boccanegra. Welcomed by Amelia, the doge discloses that the Grimaldis, her noble protectors, have been pardoned; gratefully the girl tells him of Gabriele's love, recalling her lonely past and showing him a locket that contains the portrait of her dead mother. The doge realizes that Amelia is his daughter and joyfully embraces her. When she retires, Paolo bursts in, expecting Simon to grant him Amelia's hand. Boccanegra tells him this can never be, and Paolo turns to Pietro and plots to abduct the girl when she takes her evening walk alone by the sea.

While negotiating a treaty between Genoa and Venice, the doge is interrupted by shouts outside his council chamber. In answer he grants an audience to a crowd that has captured Andrea (Fiesco) and Gabriele, who charges the doge with Amelia's abduction. As he tries to stab Boccanegra, Amelia intervenes and pleads with the doge to spare Gabriele, who now suspects she is Boccanegra's mistress. When Amelia describes her abduction, hinting at Paolo's complicity, the doge quiets the raging spectators by appealing to their higher instincts. He then commands Paolo, as a state official, to curse the man who plotted the infamy; terrified, Paolo obeys, imprecating himself. "Andrea" and Gabriele are held in custody for plotting against the doge. [This Council Chamber Scene was the only major addition in Verdi and Boito's 1881 revision of the opera.]

ACT II.   In the doge's apartment, the vengeful Paolo pours poison into Boccanegra's drinking cup. When Pietro brings "Andrea" and Gabriele from their prison cells, Paolo vainly urges the old man to assassinate Boccanegra; next he incites Gabriele with insinuations about the doge's relationship with Amelia. The youth is left to his tormented thoughts until Amelia enters, but before she can explain her love for the doge, Boccanegra is heard approaching. Gabriele hides in an alcove while Amelia asks pardon for him; the doge agrees on condition that the young man desert the conspirators. Left alone, the weary ruler drinks Paolo's potion and falls asleep. Gabriele, having overheard nothing, advances upon the doge with a knife; Amelia, however, returns in time to stop him, and at last he learns she is Boccanegra's daughter. As cries of rebellion come from below, Gabriele volunteers his services as a messenger of peace between Boccanegra and the patrician uprising. The doge consents to a marriage between Gabriele and Amelia.

ACT III.   Genoa is celebrating Boccanegra's victory over the rebels. Magnanimously he has set most of their leaders free, including "Andrea," but the traitorous Paolo has been condemned. On his way to execution, the villain informs "Andrea" that he has poisoned the doge. A captain announces that revels must end in memory of fallen heroes, after which Boccanegra, mortally ill from the poison, staggers in. "Andrea," bent on further revenge, now reveals to the doge his true identity as Fiesco, only to learn Amelia's true identity. Stunned, Fiesco tells Boccanegra that Paolo has poisoned him. As the doge dies, he blesses Gabriele and Amelia, asking that the young man be named doge. Then Fiesco announces Boccanegra's death to the people.

AROLDO

The plot of *Aroldo* is essentially identical to that of *Stiffelio* until the final scene, which, unlike *Stiffelio*'s Act III, Scene 2, is called Act IV and is not set in church. Piave has shifted the action back six hundred years to the Crusade and transferred the locale to England. Lina has become Mina, Stiffelio is Aroldo (now a knight rather than a minister), Stankar is called Egberto, Raffaele is Godvino, and Jorg Briano. Act IV takes place in Scotland, some time after the death of Godvino.

ACT IV. Aroldo and Briano live hermits' lives on the shores of Loch Lomond. They retire into their shanty after distant churchbells warrant a sunset prayer. A storm in the night beaches a boat carrying Egberto and Mina, who are rescued by villagers. Father and daughter come to the hut for shelter, but are cast out by Aroldo. Only when Briano reminds Aroldo of Christ's speech to the adulteress' accusers—"Let he that is without sin cast the first stone"—does Aroldo pardon Mina.

UN BALLO IN MASCHERA

ACT I. The scene is the Boston of 1700. Friends and courtiers of Riccardo, Earl of Warwick, Governor of Boston, await him in an audience chamber, among them a group of conspirators led by Samuel and Tom. As the governor enters, his page, Oscar, gives him the guest list for a forthcoming masked ball. Seeing the name of Amelia—wife of his secretary, Renato—he muses on his secret passion for her. As the others leave, the page admits Renato himself, who says he knows the cause of the governor's disturbed look—a conspiracy against his life. But Riccardo ignores his friend's warning. A magistrate arrives with a decree banishing the fortune-teller Ulrica, who has been accused of evil practices. When Riccardo asks Oscar's opinion, the youth proclaims her not guilty and describes her skill at stargazing. Deciding to see for himself and overruling the objections of Renato, the governor lightheartedly bids the court join him in an incognito visit to the soothsayer.

After she has muttered incantations over her caldron, Ulrica tells the sailor Silvano that he will soon prosper. Riccardo, disguised as a fisherman, surreptitiously slips money and a promotion into the pocket of the seaman, who discovers it and marvels at the fortune-teller's powers. The governor stays in hiding when Ulrica sends her visitors away to grant an audience to Amelia, who comes seeking release from her love for Riccardo. Ulrica tells her to find a magic herb that grows by the gallows; Amelia hurries away. A moment later Oscar and members of the court enter, and Riccardo, still incognito, asks Ulrica to read his palm; when she says he will die by the next hand he shakes, the governor laughs. But no one will shake his hand. Riccardo sees Renato, who arrives too late to hear Ulrica, and clasps his hand. Riccardo is recognized and hailed by the crowd.

ACT II.   Amelia arrives at the gloomy gallows and desperately prays that the herb she seeks there will release her from her passion for the governor. As a distant bell tolls midnight, she is terrified by a shadowy figure, which turns out to be Riccardo. Unable to resist his ardent words, Amelia confesses she loves him but quickly veils her face when her husband rushes in to warn the governor to flee approaching assassins. Riccardo, fearing that Renato may discover Amelia's identity, leaves only after his secretary promises to escort her back to the city without lifting her veil. Finding the governor's secretary instead of their intended victim, the conspirators curse their luck. Renato draws his sword when they make insolent remarks about his veiled companion; to save her husband's life, Amelia raises her veil. While the conspirators laugh at this irony, Renato asks their two leaders to come to his house that night.

ACT III. Dragging Amelia into their home, Renato tells her that he intends to kill her; Amelia asks to see her young son before she dies. Granting her wish, Renato turns to curse a portrait of Riccardo. He is interrupted by Samuel and Tom; now united in purpose, they cannot agree who should have the privilege of assassinating the governor. Amelia returns just as the men prepare to draw lots. Forcing his wife to take the fatal slip from a vase, Renato rejoices when she draws his name. A moment later Oscar brings an invitation to the masked ball. While the men hail this chance to execute their plan, Amelia decides to warn Riccardo.

Alone in his apartment, Riccardo renounces his love, resolving to send Amelia and Renato to England. Oscar delivers a letter to the governor from an unknown lady, warning him of the murder plot; but not wanting his absence to be taken as a sign of cowardice, Riccardo leaves for the masquerade.

In the ballroom, festivities are in progress. The three conspirators wander through the throng trying to learn the disguise of the governor. Renato, taking Oscar aside, attempts to persuade the youth to reveal the information and obtains it only after playful evasions. Recognizing Amelia, Riccardo speaks with her; despite her repeated warning, he refuses to leave. Just as the lovers bid a final farewell, Renato, overhearing the last part of their conversation, plunges his dagger into the governor. The dying Riccardo, surrounded by his court, forgives Renato, who learns too late of his wife's innocence.

Before the Papal censor in Rome decreed that the opera must take place in a non-European country, *Un Ballo in Maschera* was set in Sweden in 1792. Riccardo was King Gustavus III of Sweden, Renato his first minister Anckarstrom; the conspirators were Counts Ribbing and Warting and Ulrica had a last name, Arvidson. The ballroom scene was set in Stockholm's Royal Opera House.

LA FORZA DEL DESTINO

ACT I.   In his palace in mid-eighteenth century Seville, the Marquis of
Calatrava bids goodnight to his daughter, Leonora. He warns her against
her suitor, Don Alvaro, an Inca prince, and is hardly out the door when
Curra, a maid, prepares for Leonora's elopement with Alvaro. But Leonora
isn't sure she wants to go through with it until Alvaro arrives at the
balcony window and convinces her anew. Suddenly, the Marquis storms
in, his sword drawn. Alvaro, to make peace, throws down his pistol,
which accidentally goes off and wounds the Marquis, who dies, cursing
his daughter. The lovers flee together.

ACT II.   Separated from Alvaro during their escape, Leonora, in male
attire, is now in flight from her vengeful brother, Carlo. Brother and
sister turn up at the same village inn, but Carlo doesn't recognize her.
A lively gypsy named Preziosilla regales the crowd with a hymn to war,
and Leonora leaves with some passing pilgrims. After annoying the
peddler Trabuco with his questions, Carlo tells his own story, pretending
it happened to someone else. He is still unaware that he just missed finding his sister.

   Shortly thereafter, Leonora seeks refuge at a Franciscan monastery. She
prays to the Virgin for forgiveness and asks the talkative friar Melitone
if she may speak with the father superior. With compassion, the Padre
Guardiano offers Leonora sanctuary. Other monks join in prayer and
Leonora goes off to an isolated cave to spend her life in penitence.

ACT III.   Alvaro has joined the Spanish army in Italy under an alias.
Believing Leonora dead, he broods on his past. When the sound of
quarreling over cards brings him to a nearby tavern, he rescues a fellow
officer from a brawl. It is Leonora's brother, Carlo, also disguised. The
two pledge undying friendship.

In the morning, while putting the Germans to rout, Alvaro is gravely wounded. Carlo offers him the Calatrava medal, but Alvaro refuses violently, causing Carlo to suspect that Alvaro is the man he is hunting. While the surgeon tries to save Alvaro, Carlo wrestles with his conscience, only to give in and go look among Alvaro's belongings, where he finds Leonora's portrait. When the surgeon announces that Alvaro will live, Carlo rejoices that he can now confront his enemy.

A few months later, as day dawns, Carlo finds Alvaro and reveals his identity to the healed and healthy officer, challenging him to a duel. Alvaro tries to pacify him until he hears that Leonora lives—and Carlo intends to kill her. But the patrol separates them as they come to blows; Alvaro resolves to end his worldly suffering in a monastery. The stage fills with the flotsam and jetsam of wartime: soldiers, camp followers, beggars, frightened recruits, Trabuco again and Brother Melitone, who lectures everyone on their amoral behavior. They chase him off and join Preziosilla in a rataplan.

ACT IV.   Back at the Franciscan sanctum, Melitone grudgingly doles out soup to beggars while Padre Guardiano reminds him to be more humble. Carlo enters, having tracked his prey here, but the peaceful Alvaro refuses to fight him until goaded by an insult to his race. They rush off to duel.

In a nearby grotto Leonora prays to God for peace. She still loves Alvaro and longs for death. When sounds of fighting disturb her she hides in her cave, cursing the intruders. Carlo's voice is heard calling for absolution. Alvaro runs in; seeing the hermit's door, he pounds on it, pleading for help for the dying man—and finds himself facing Leonora. He speeds her to her dying brother, but Carlo cannot forgive her even now: he stabs her, and she staggers back to die in the arms of Padre Guardiano, who tells the surviving Alvaro to look to God for salvation.

DON CARLOS

ACT I. 1568.   Don Carlo, Infante of Spain, has traveled incognito with the Spanish ambassador's retinue into the forest of Fontainebleau, hoping to catch sight of his intended, French princess Elisabeth de Valois. He is very pleased with her gentility and beauty when her suite passes by and she hands out alms to the foresters. Meanwhile, night has fallen and Carlo has lost his party; so has Elisabeth, who returns escorted by her page. Don Carlo steps forth and offers to protect her while the page goes off to Fontainebleau to fetch help. Carlo discloses that a peace treaty between France and Spain is expected to be signed that night and sealed with a marriage between the royal houses. Elisabeth fears her fiancé will not return her love, but Carlo allays all doubt by giving her a portrait of the Infante—himself—and proclaiming his love. Their excited vision of the future collapses when the page returns to hail Elisabeth as Queen of Spain. She protests: she is to marry the Infante; but her father, Henry II, has pledged her to Carlo's father, Philip II of Spain. She must accept. The lovers' lamentations are swallowed in rejoicing as the royal suite moves on to the château.

ACT II.   At the monastery of St. Just, monks pray at the tomb of Charles V. Carlo, who comes in search of consolation, is terrified by a mysterious friar's resemblance to his late grandfather. The prince is soon joined by Rodrigo, Marquess of Posa, who urges him to leave for the Netherlands, both to cure himself of his infatuation for his stepmother and to protect Flanders from Spanish tyranny. The two friends dedicate themselves to the cause of freedom. As Philip and Elisabeth pass, Carlo is seized anew with love for Elisabeth.

In the cloister garden a group of ladies and their pages hear Princess Eboli sing a Moorish song. The queen enters sadly, followed shortly by

Rodrigo, who begs her to see the prince. The other ladies retire. Carlo asks the queen to help him obtain Philip's leave to go to Flanders, but then, overcome with passion, falls at her feet. After Elisabeth sends Carlo away, Philip suddenly enters with his court and, finding his wife alone, banishes the Countess of Aremberg for not attending the queen; Elisabeth consoles the distraught woman, with whom she withdraws. Rodrigo remains to plead the Flemish cause with Philip, who suspects that his wife and son are lovers and asks Rodrigo to spy on them. He also warns him to beware of the Grand Inquisitor, enemy of the Protestant Flemish.

ACT III. At midnight in the castle gardens in Madrid, Carlo reads a note that he believes is from Elisabeth but which in reality comes from Eboli, who also loves him. When the veiled Eboli enters, Carlo, thinking her the queen, speaks his heart; Eboli unveils, and both realize their error. As Eboli furiously accuses the prince of loving Elisabeth, Rodrigo enters. Carlo has to restrain his friend from slaying Eboli, who swears to expose the lovers. When the Princess is gone, Rodrigo implores Carlo to leave his documents with him lest they incriminate the prince. Reluctant though he is to do so, having heard of Rodrigo's intimacy with Philip, Carlo is persuaded by a reminder of their earlier oath of friendship.

In the square before Our Lady of Atocha Cathedral, an immense crowd assembles to watch the burning of a band of heretics. When the king emerges from the church, he is halted by six Flemish deputies, led by Carlo, who plead for mercy. The friars, however, insist on punishment of the rebellious subjects. Carlo swears to champion the Flemish cause, defying his father, who orders him disarmed. To Carlo's surprise, it is Rodrigo who obeys the king's command. As the auto-da-fé begins, a voice from heaven proclaims the innocents saved.

ACT IV. In his study, Philip laments the queen's indifference and his own inability to understand the human heart. At the king's request, the aged, blind Grand Inquisitor comes in to discuss matters of state; he urges the death of both Carlo and Rodrigo on grounds of treason. As the old man leaves, the king muses ruefully that the throne must always yield to the demands of the altar. Elisabeth suddenly bursts in, crying that her jewel casket has been stolen, at which Philip ironically hands it to her; when she hesitates, he breaks the lock himself, revealing a portrait of Carlo. Elisabeth, who reminds him that she was once betrothed to the prince, faints at his accusation of adultery. The king's call for help brings Eboli and Rodrigo. After the two men depart, Eboli tells Elisabeth that jealousy made her give the casket to Philip, adding that she herself was once the king's mistress. Banishing the princess to a convent, Elisabeth leaves. Eboli, cursing her own fatal beauty, resolves to save Carlo's life.

Rodrigo visits Carlo's cell to relate that he has assumed full blame for the revolution in Flanders; he urges his friend to take heart and lead the cause of freedom. A bullet fired by a soldier of the Inquisition kills Rodrigo. A moment later the king enters to release Carlo from prison, but son denounces father as a murderer. When a mob storms the prison to attack Philip, the Grand Inquisitor steps forward, silencing the crowd and saving the crown. In the tumult, Eboli presses Carlo to flee.

ACT V.   Back in the Monastery of St. Just, the miserable Elisabeth waits to bid Carlo farewell. The prince enters and tells her he leaves to further the Flemish cause. Surprised by Philip and the Inquisitor, Carlo is saved from arrest by the ghost of Charles V, who emerges from his tomb and draws his grandson into the shadows.

AIDA

ACT I.   The Age of the Pharaohs. In the royal palace at Memphis, Radames, a young captain of the guard, learns from the high priest, Ramfis, that Ethiopia threatens the Nile valley. Alone, Radames hopes to be chosen army commander, envisioning a glorious victory so he can free his beloved Aida—the Ethiopian slave of Amneris, the king's daughter.

Amneris, who herself loves Radames, appears and questions him; she senses his feelings for Aida, especially as the girl enters. Soon the royal procession arrives to hear a messenger confirm that the Ethiopian army, led by Amonasro, is marching on Thebes. The king announces Radames' appointment. "Return victorious!" cries Amneris, echoed by the people. Left alone, Aida repeats these words, stunned that the man she loves is going to battle her father—for she is a princess of Ethiopia, daughter of Amonasro. Torn by conflicting loyalties, she begs the gods for pity.

In the Temple of Ptah, a priestess is heard addressing the deity while a ceremonial dance is performed. Ramfis consecrates Radames' sword for the campaign.

ACT II.   Radames has beaten the Ethiopians, and on the morning of his triumphal return Amneris is groomed by slaves and diverted from her romantic daydreaming by dancers. At Aida's approach she dismisses her attendants, tricking the girl by pretending Radames is dead, then saying he lives. Certain from Aida's reaction that her slave does love Radames, Amneris threatens her and leaves for the festivities.

At the gate of Thebes, a crowd welcomes the returning army; the defeat of the Ethiopians is celebrated in parade and dance. Radames is borne in and crowned with a victor's wreath by Amneris. The captured Ethiopians follow, among them Aida's father, Amonasro, incognito. When Aida calls out to him, he warns her in an aside not to betray his rank, then pleads for the lives of his fellow prisoners. Ramfis and the priests command death for the captives, but Radames intercedes, requiring their freedom as his reward. The king releases all but Amonasro, then presents Radames with the hand of Amneris, dashing Aida's dreams of happiness.

ACT III.   On a moonlit bank of the Nile, Ramfis leads Amneris into a temple of Isis for a wedding vigil. Aida comes to wait secretly for Radames; overcome with nostalgia, she laments her conquered homeland. Amonasro startles her out of her reverie, still determined to save his people: Aida must trick Radames into revealing where the Egyptian army intends to enter Ethiopia. He shames and threatens her, finally breaking down her resistance. Amonasro hides as Radames appears, ardent with promises to make Aida his bride after his next victory. She suggests they run away together, asking what route his army will take. No sooner has he answered than Amonasro steps out, triumphantly divulging his identity as king of Ethiopia. Leaving the temple, Amneris finds them all and denounces Radames as a traitor. Amonasro lunges at her with a dagger, but Radames shields her and surrenders himself to Ramfis as Aida and her father escape.

ACT IV. When Radames is led into the temple of judgment, Amneris offers to save him if he will renounce Aida. This he says he will never do. Enraged, Amneris sends him to his doom, listening in despair as the priests three times demand that he defend himself and are thrice met with silence. Amneris' pride falls away, her love for Radames revealed by her agony in hearing him condemned by the priests, whom she curses when they file past.

Radames, buried alive in a crypt beneath the temple, turns his last thoughts to Aida, who emerges from the shadows, having entered the vault earlier to share his fate. Radames tries vainly to dislodge the stone that locks them in. Bidding farewell to earth, the vale of tears, the lovers greet eternity as the penitent Amneris prays above them for Radames' soul.

OTELLO

ACT I. As a tempest rages in the harbor of fifteenth-century Cyprus, citizens await the return of their governor, Otello, a Moorish general in the Venetian army. When his ship is sighted, the Cypriots call on heaven to spare it. Safely in port, Otello stops on the ramparts to proclaim victory over the Turks and then enters his castle. His ensign Iago, angered because a rival, Cassio, has been promoted to captain, plots his own advancement by fanning the secret desires of Roderigo for Otello's wife, Desdemona. Leading the Cypriots in a drinking song around a bonfire, Iago forces the easily intoxicated Cassio to drink toasts to Otello and his bride; the ensign next provokes Roderigo to duel with the reeling Cassio. Otello's predecessor, Montano, tries to intervene but is wounded by Cassio. Suddenly Otello, awakened by the brawl, storms out to demand an explanation; Iago pretends ignorance. As Desdemona joins her husband, he demotes Cassio, instructing Iago to restore order. Otello, left alone with Desdemona in the moonlight, tenderly recalls their courtship and plucks a kiss from her lips.

ACT II.   On a terrace, Iago advises Cassio to seek Desdemona's aid in regaining Otello's favor. Cassio goes off, leaving Iago to describe his view of his creator, a cruel demon who inspires his evil machinations. On Otello's arrival, he makes innuendos about Desdemona's fidelity as they spy her in the garden with Emilia (Iago's wife) and Cassio; he warns the Moor to beware of jealousy. Women, children and sailors bring flowers to Desdemona, whose beauty softens Otello's suspicions, but when she approaches him about Cassio's reinstatement, he grows irritable. Fearing he is ill, she tries to soothe his brow with a handkerchief, which he throws to the ground. Desdemona, confused, pleads her devotion, while Iago wrenches the handkerchief from Emilia, who has retrieved it. When the women leave, Otello accuses his ensign of destroying his peace of mind and demands proof of his wife's faithlessness. Iago pretends he has heard Cassio murmur Desdemona's name in his sleep; even worse, he has seen in Cassio's hand the handkerchief Otello gave her when he first courted her. Otello vows vengeance, seconded by Iago.

ACT III.   In the armory, Iago tells Otello that more proof is forthcoming and then departs as Desdemona greets her husband. The Moor hints at his suspicions, but she fails to understand; when he demands the handkerchief he once gave her, she again pleads for Cassio. Infuriated, Otello calls her a courtesan. She swears her innocence through tears, but is reviled and sent away. Spent with rage, Otello muses on his misery, then hides at the approach of Cassio and Iago. The ensign, flashing the handkerchief he stole, manipulates Cassio's banter about his mistress, Bianca, so that Otello thinks they mean Desdemona. Cassio leaves as trumpets announce dignitaries from Venice. Otello determines to kill his wife that night and promotes Iago to captain.

In the great hall of the castle, the court enters to welcome Lodovico, the ambassador, who presents papers recalling Otello to Venice and naming Cassio governor. When Cassio steps forward, Otello loses self-control and, cursing Desdemona, hurls her to the floor. She begs forgiveness for her supposed crime; the courtiers try to console her, but Otello orders them all out. As the Moor falls unconscious in a fit, Iago mockingly hails the so-called Lion of Venice.

ACT IV. In her room, as Emilia helps her prepare for bed, Desdemona sings a song about a maiden forsaken by her lover. She bids her companion an emphatic good night, says her prayers and retires. Otello soon steals in and tenderly kisses her. When she awakens, he tells her to prepare for death; though she protests her innocence, he strangles her. Suddenly Emilia knocks with news that Cassio has slain Roderigo. Hearing Desdemona's death moan, she cries for help, bringing Iago, Lodovico and Cassio. Emilia tells of Iago's treachery, but the villain escapes, stabbing his wife. Otello, realizing he has been duped, stabs himself and dies upon a final kiss.

FALSTAFF

ACT I. The reign of Henry IV. Sir John Falstaff, the portly rascal of Windsor, sits in the Garter Inn with his "bad companions" Bardolfo and Pistola. When Dr. Caius enters to accuse the three of abusing his home and robbing him, Falstaff dismisses the charges with mock solemnity. He then upbraids his friends for being unable to pay the bill. Seeking to better his fortunes, Falstaff plans to woo two wealthy matrons, Alice Ford and Meg Page; he produces love letters to both ladies, but his henchmen decide their ethics forbid them to deliver them. Falstaff gives the notes to a page boy and lectures his cronies on honor, driving his point home with a broomstick as he chases them from the inn.

In her garden, Alice and her daughter Nannetta talk to Meg and Dame Quickly, soon discovering that Falstaff has sent identical letters. Outraged, they resolve to punish him, then withdraw as Ford arrives with Caius, Fenton, Bardolfo and Pistola, all warning him about Falstaff's designs. Briefly alone, Nannetta and Fenton steal kisses until the women return, plotting to send Quickly to Falstaff to arrange a rendezvous with Alice. Nannetta and Fenton are again interrupted, this time by Ford, who also plans to visit Falstaff. As the women reappear, all pledge to take the fat knight down a peg or two.

ACT II. At the inn, Falstaff accepts Bardolfo and Pistola's feigned penitence for their mutiny. Soon Quickly curtsies in to assure the knight that both Alice and Meg return his ardor. Arranging a meeting with Alice, Falstaff rewards Quickly with a pittance and then, alone, preens himself. The next visitor is Ford, disguised as "Signor Fontana" and proclaiming an unrequited passion for Alice. Employed to break down the lady's virtue, Falstaff boasts that he has already set up a tryst and steps out to array himself. Ford, unable to believe his ears, vows to avenge his honor. Falstaff returns, his toilette complete, and the two exit.

In Ford's house, Quickly tells Alice and Meg about her visit with the knight at the inn. Nannetta does not share in the fun: her father has promised her to Caius. The women reassure her and hide as Alice sits strumming a lute for the arrival of her corpulent suitor. Recalling his salad days as a slender page, he is cut short when Quickly announces

Meg's imminent approach. Falstaff leaps behind a screen, and Meg sails in to report that Ford is on his way over in a fury. Quickly confirms this, and while Ford and his men search the house Falstaff takes refuge with the dirty linen in a laundry basket. Slipping behind the screen, Nannetta and Fenton attract attention with the sound of their kissing. While Meg and Quickly muffle Falstaff's cries for air, Ford sneaks up on the screen and knocks it over, expecting to uncover his wife with Falstaff. But Alice is ordering servants to heave the basket into the Thames, and she leads her husband to the window to see Falstaff drag himself from the river.

ACT III. At sunset, outside the inn, Falstaff bemoans his misadventure while downing a mug of warm wine. His reflections are halted by Quickly, who insists that Alice still loves him and proves it with a note appointing a midnight rendezvous in Windsor Park. Alice, Ford, Meg, Caius and Fenton sneak in as Falstaff enters the inn with Quickly, who eagerly tells him the gory tale of the Black Huntsman's ghost, often seen in Windsor Park at night. Alice and the others take up the story and plot to frighten Falstaff by dressing up as wood sprites. As the conspirators disband, Quickly overhears Ford promise Nannetta in marriage to Caius.

In moonlit Windsor forest, Fenton sings of love and receives a monk's costume for the masquerade; Nannetta is queen of the fairies, Meg a nymph and Quickly a witch. Everyone takes off as Falstaff lumbers in, got up as a huntsman and wearing antlers. Scarcely has he greeted Alice than Meg warns of approaching demons. As the knight cowers, Nannetta calls the forest creatures to their revels, mainly tormenting Falstaff until he begs for mercy. When the tricksters unmask, Sir John takes it like a sport. Ford betrothes Caius to the queen of the fairies (Bardolfo in Nannetta's costume) and unwittingly blesses Nannetta and Fenton. Now Ford too has been duped, but he can forgive as well, and the entire company celebrates with laughter.

WORLD PREMIERES AND METROPOLITAN OPERA PREMIERES

OBERTO, CONTE DE SAN BONIFACIO

Teatro alla Scala, Milan
November 17, 1839
OBERTO: Ignazio Marini
LEONORA: Antonietta Raineri-Marini
RICCARDO: Lorenzo Salvi
CUNIZA: Maria Shaw
CONDUCTED BY Eugenio Cavallini

UN GIORNO DI REGNO
(Il Finto Stanislao)

Teatro alla Scala, Milan
September 5, 1840
MARCHESA: Antonietta Raineri-Marini
EDOARDO: Lorenzo Salvi
GIULIETTA: Luigia Abbadia
BELFIORE: Raffaele Ferlotti
KELBAR: Raffaele Scalese
LA ROCCA: Agostino Rovere
CONDUCTED BY Eugenio Cavallini

NABUCODONOSOR
(Nabucco)

Teatro alla Scala, Milan
March 9, 1842
NABUCCO: Giorgio Ronconi
ABIGAILLE: Giuseppina Strepponi
ISMAELE: Corrado Miraglia
FENENA: Giovannina Bellinzaghi
ZACCARIA: Prosper Dérivis
HIGH PRIEST: Gaetano Rossi
CONDUCTED BY Eugenio Cavallini

Metropolitan Opera, New York
October 24, 1960
NABUCCO: Cornell MacNeil
ABIGAILLE: Leonie Rysanek
ISMAELE: Eugenio Fernandi
FENENA: Rosalind Elias
ZACCARIA: Cesare Siepi
HIGH PRIEST: Bonaldo Giaiotti
CONDUCTED BY Thomas Schippers

I LOMBARDI ALLA PRIMA CROCIATA

Teatro alla Scala, Milan
February 11, 1843
GISELDA: Erminia Frezzolini-Poggi
ORONTE: Carlo Guasco
PAGANO: Prosper Dérivis
ARVINO: Giovanni Severi
CONDUCTED BY Eugenio Cavallini

ERNANI

Teatro la Fenice, Venice
March 9, 1844
ERNANI: Carlo Guasco
ELVIRA: Sophie Löwe
DON CARLO: Antonio Superchi
SILVA: Antonio Selva
CONDUCTED BY Gaetano Mares

Metropolitan Opera, New York
January 28, 1903
ERNANI: Emilio De Marchi
ELVIRA: Marcella Sembrich
DON CARLO: Antonio Scotti
SILVA: Edouard De Reszke
CONDUCTED BY Luigi Mancinelli

I DUE FOSCARI

Teatro Argentina, Rome
November 3, 1844
JACOPO FOSCARI: Giacomo Roppa
FRANCESCO FOSCARI: Achille De Bassini
LUCREZIA CONTERINI: Marianna Barbieri-Nini
JACOPO LOREDANO: Baldassare Mirri
CONDUCTED BY Giovani Nostini

GIOVANNA D'ARCO

Teatro alla Scala, Milan
February 15, 1845
GIOVANNA: Erminia Frezzolini-Poggi
CARLO VII: Antonio Poggi
GIACOMO: Filippo Colini
CONDUCTED BY Eugenio Cavallini

ALZIRA

Teatro San Carlo, Naples
August 12, 1845
ALZIRA: Eugenia Tadolini
ZAMORO: Gaetano Fraschini
GUSMANO: Filippo Coletti
ALVARO: Marco Arati
CONDUCTED BY Antonio Farelli

ATTILA

Teatro la Fenice, Venice
March 17, 1846
ATTILA: Ignazio Marini
ODABELLA: Sophie Löwe
FORESTO: Carlo Guasco
EZIO: Natale Costantini
CONDUCTED BY Gaetano Mares

MACBETH

Teatro della Pergola, Florence
March 14, 1847
MACBETH: Felice Varesi
LADY MACBETH: Marianna Barbieri-Nini
BANQUO: Nicola Benedetti
MACDUFF: Angelo Brunacci
CONDUCTED BY Giuseppe Verdi

Théâtre Lyrique Impérial, Paris
April 21, 1865 (Revised, in French)
MACBETH: Jean-Vital-Ismael Jammes
LADY MACBETH: Mme. Rey-Balla
BANQUO: Bilis Petit
MACDUFF: Jules Monjauze
CONDUCTED BY M. Deloffre

Metropolitan Opera, New York
February 5, 1959
MACBETH: Leonard Warren
LADY MACBETH: Leonie Rysanek
BANQUO: Jerome Hines
MACDUFF: Carlo Bergonzi
CONDUCTED BY Erich Leinsdorf

I MASNADIERI

Her Majesty's Theatre, London
July 22, 1847
AMALIA: Jenny Lind
CARLO: Italo Gardoni
FRANCESCO: Filippo Coletti
MASSIMILIANO: Luigi Lablache
ARMINIO: Leone Corelli
MOSER: Lucien Bouché
CONDUCTED BY Giuseppe Verdi

JERUSALEM
(revision of *I Lombardi*)

Académie Royale de Musique, Paris
November 26, 1847
HÉLÈNE: Esther Elisa Julian-Van Gelder
GASTON: Gilbert Louis Duprez
COMTE: Charles Portheaut
ROGER: Adolphe Louis Joseph Alizard
CONDUCTED BY Narcisse Girard

IL CORSARO

Teatro Grande, Trieste
October 25, 1848
CORRADO: Gaetano Fraschini
MEDORA: Carolina Rapazzini
GULNARA: Marianna Barbieri-Nini
SEID: Achille De Bassini
CONDUCTED BY Giuseppe Alessandro Scaramelli

LA BATTAGLIA DI LEGNANO

Teatro Argentina, Rome
January 27, 1849
LIDA: Teresa De Giuli-Borsi
ARRIGO: Gaetano Fraschini
ROLANDO: Filippo Colini
BARBAROSSA: Pietro Sottovia
CONDUCTED BY Emilo Angelini

LUISA MILLER

Teatro San Carlo, Naples
December 8, 1849
LUISA: Marietta Gazzaniga-Malaspina
RODOLFO: Settimio Malvezzi
MILLER: Achille De Bassini
WALTER: Antonio Selva
WURM: Marco Arati
FEDERICA: Teresa Della Salandri
CONDUCTED BY Antonio Farelli

Metropolitan Opera, New York
December 21, 1929
LUISA: Rosa Ponselle
RODOLFO: Giacomo Lauri-Volpi
MILLER: Giuseppe De Luca
WALTER: Tancredi Pasero
WURM: Pavel Ludikar
FEDERICA: Marion Telva
CONDUCTED BY Tullio Serafin

STIFFELIO

Teatro Grande, Trieste
November 16, 1850
STIFFELIO: Gaetano Fraschini
LINA: Marietta Gazzaniga-Malaspina
STANKAR: Filippo Colini
RAFFAELE: Raineri Dei
JORG: Francesco Reduzzi
CONDUCTED BY Giuseppe Verdi
CONDUCTED BY Giuseppe Alessandro Scaramelli

RIGOLETTO

Teatro la Fenice, Venice
March 11, 1851
RIGOLETTO: Felice Varesi
GILDA: Teresina Brambilla
DUKE OF MANTUA: Raffaele Mirate
SPARAFUCILE: Feliciano Ponz
MADDALENA: Annetta Casaloni
CONDUCTED BY Carlo Ercole Bosoni

Metropolitan Opera, New York
November 16, 1883
RIGOLETTO: Luigi Guadagnini
GILDA: Marcella Sembrich
DUKE OF MANTUA: Roberto Stagno
SPARAFUCILE: Franco Novara
MADDALENA: Sofia Scalchi
CONDUCTED BY Auguste Vianesi

IL TROVATORE

Teatro Apollo, Rome
January 19, 1853
MANRICO: Carlo Boucardé
LEONORA: Rosina Penco
AZUCENA: Emilia Goggi
DI LUNA: Giovanni Guicciardi
FERRANDO: Arcangelo Balderi
CONDUCTED BY Emilo Angelini

Metropolitan Opera, New York
October 26, 1883
MANRICO: Roberto Stagno
LEONORA: Alwina Valleria
AZUCENA: Zelia Trebelli
DI LUNA: Giuseppe Kaschmann
FERRANDO: Achille Augier
CONDUCTED BY Auguste Vianesi

LA TRAVIATA

Teatro la Fenice, Venice
March 6, 1853
VIOLETTA: Fanny Salvini-Donatelli
ALFREDO: Lodovico Graziani
GERMONT: Felice Varesi
CONDUCTED BY Gaetano Mares

Metropolitan Opera, New York
November 5, 1883
VIOLETTA: Marcella Sembrich
ALFREDO: Victor Capoul
GERMONT: Giuseppe Del Puente
CONDUCTED BY Auguste Vianesi

LES VÊPRES SICILIENNES

Salle Le Peletier, Paris
June 13, 1855
HÉLÈNE: Sophie Cruvelli
HENRI: Louis Guéymard
MONFORT: Marc Bonnehée
PROCIDA: Louis-Henri Obin
CONDUCTED BY Narcisse Girard

Metropolitan Opera, New York
January 31, 1974 (in Italian)
ELENA: Montserrat Caballé
ARRIGO: Nicolai Gedda
MONFORTE: Sherrill Milnes
PROCIDA: Justino Díaz
CONDUCTED BY James Levine

SIMON BOCCANEGRA

Teatro la Fenice, Venice
March 12, 1857
BOCCANEGRA: Leone Giraldoni
MARIA: Luigia Bendazzi
GABRIELE: Carlo Negrini
FIESCO: Giuseppe Echeverria
PAOLO: Giacomo Vercellini
CONDUCTED BY Carlo Ercole Bosoni

Teatro alla Scala, Milan
March 24, 1881 (Revised)
BOCCANEGRA: Victor Maurel
MARIA: Anna D'Angeri
GABRIELE: Francesco Tamagno
FIESCO: Edoard De Reszke
PAOLO: Federico Salvati
CONDUCTED BY Franco Faccio

Metropolitan Opera, New York
January 28, 1932
BOCCANEGRA: Lawrence Tibbett
MARIA: Maria Müller
GABRIELE: Giovanni Martinelli
FIESCO: Ezio Pinza
PAOLO: Claudio Frigerio
CONDUCTED BY Tullio Serafin

AROLDO

(revision of *Stiffelio*)

Teatro Nuovo, Rimini
August 16, 1857
AROLDO: Emilio Pancani
MINA: Marcellina Lotti della Santa
EGBERTO: Gaetano Ferri
BRIANO: Giovanni Battista Cornago
GODVINO: Salvatore Poggiali
CONDUCTED BY Angelo Mariani

UN BALLO IN MASCHERA

Teatro Apollo, Rome
February 17, 1859
AMELIA: Eugenia Julienne-Dejean
RICCARDO: Gaetano Fraschini
RENATO: Leone Giraldoni
ULRICA: Zelinda Sbriscia
OSCAR: Pamela Scotti
SAMUELE: Cesare Bossi
TOMMASO: Giovanni Bernardoni
CONDUCTED BY Emilio Angelini

Metropolitan Opera, New York
December 11, 1889 (in German)
AMELIA: Lilli Lehmann
RICCARDO: Julius Perotti
RENATO: Theodore Reichmann
ULRICA: Emmy Sonntag-Uhl
OSCAR: Betty Frank
SAMUELE: Josef Arden
TOMMASO: Conrad Behrens
CONDUCTED BY Anton Seidl

LA FORZA DEL DESTINO

Imperial Theatre, St. Petersburg
November 10, 1862
LEONORA: Carolina Barbot
DON ALVARO: Enrico Tamberlik
DON CARLO: Francesco Graziani
PADRE GUARDIANO: Gian Francesco Angelini
PREZIOSILLA: Constance Nantier-Didiée
MELITONE: Achille De Bassini
CONDUCTED BY Sig. Baveri

Metropolitan Opera, New York
November 15, 1918
LEONORA: Rosa Ponselle
DON ALVARO: Enrico Caruso
DON CARLO: Giuseppe De Luca
PADRE GUARDIANO: José Mardones
PREZIOSILLA: Alice Gentle
MELITONE: Thomas Chalmers
CONDUCTED BY Gennaro Papi

DON CARLOS

Théâtre de l'Opéra, Paris
March 11, 1867
DON CARLOS: A. Morère
ELISABETH: Marie-Constance Sass
PHILIPPE II: Louis-Henri Obin
EBOLI: Pauline Guéymard-Lauters
RODRIGUE: Jean-Baptiste Faure
INQUISITEUR: M. David
CONDUCTED BY Georges François Hainl

Metropolitan Opera, New York
December 23, 1920 (in Italian)
DON CARLO: Giovanni Martinelli
ELISABETTA: Rosa Ponselle
FILIPPO II: Adamo Didur
EBOLI: Margarete Matzenauer
RODRIGO: Giuseppe De Luca
INQUISITORE: Louis D'Angelo
CONDUCTED BY Gennaro Papi

AIDA

Italian Theater, Cairo
December 24, 1871
AIDA: Antonietta Pozzoni-Anastasi
RADAMES: Pietro Mongini
AMNERIS: Eleonora Grossi
AMONASRO: Francesco Steller
RAMFIS: Paolo Medini
KING: Tommaso Costa
CONDUCTED BY Giovanni Bottesini

Metropolitan Opera, New York
November 12, 1886 (in German)
AIDA: Therese Herbert-Förster
RADAMES: Carl Zobel
AMNERIS: Marianne Brandt
AMONASRO: Adolf Robinson
RAMFIS: Emil Fischer
KING: George Sieglitz
CONDUCTED BY Anton Seidl

MESSA DA REQUIEM

Chiesa San Marco, Milan
May 22, 1874
SOPRANO: Teresa Stolz
MEZZO-SOPRANO: Maria Waldmann
TENOR: Giuseppe Capponi
BASS: Ormondo Maini
CONDUCTED BY Giuseppe Verdi

Metropolitan Opera, New York
February 17, 1901
SOPRANO: Lillian Nordica
MEZZO-SOPRANO: Ernestine Schumann-Heink
TENOR: Thomas Salignac
BASS: Pol Plançon
CONDUCTED BY Luigi Mancinelli

OTELLO

Teatro alla Scala, Milan
February 5, 1887
OTELLO: Francesco Tamagno
DESDEMONA: Romilda Pantaleoni
IAGO: Victor Maurel
EMILIA: Ginevra Petrovich
CASSIO: Giovanni Paroli
LODOVICO: Francesco Navarini
CONDUCTED BY Franco Faccio

Metropolitan Opera, New York
January 11, 1891
OTELLO: Jean De Reszke
DESDEMONA: Emma Albani
IAGO: Eduardo Camera
EMILIA: Sofia Scalchi
CASSIO: Victor Capoul
LODOVICO: Enrico Serbolini
CONDUCTED BY Louis Saar

FALSTAFF

Teatro alla Scala, Milan
February 9, 1893
FALSTAFF: Victor Maurel
ALICE: Emma Zilli
FORD: Antonio Pini-Corsi
QUICKLY: Giuseppina Pasqua
MEG: Virginia Guerrini
NANNETTA: Adelina Stehle
FENTON: Edoardo Garbin
CONDUCTED BY Edoardo Mascheroni

Metropolitan Opera, New York
February 4, 1895
FALSTAFF: Victor Maurel
ALICE: Emma Eames
FORD: Giuseppe Campanari
QUICKLY: Sofia Scalchi
MEG: Jane De Vigne
NANNETTA: Zélie De Lussan
FENTON: Giuseppe Russitano
CONDUCTED BY Luigi Mancinelli